DATE DUE

HOME HOLD LOVER'S

RARY DIST.
81631

PULCRUM PUBLISHING
GOLDEN, COLORADO

WITHDRAWN

ISBN 1-55591-494-2
ISSN 1544-3787

Editorial: Marlene Blessing, Daniel Forrest-Bank, Alison Auch
Cover and interior design: Anne Clark
Lower left cover image: Copyright © Charles Mann, garden owner/designer: Ann Anderson (Denver).

Printed in Singapore
0 9 8 7 6 5 4 3 2 1

Fulcrum Publishing
16100 Table Mountain Parkway, Suite 300
Golden, Colorado 80403
(800) 992-2908 • (303) 277-1623
www.fulcrum-books.com

■ Rustic Gems: Colorado Cabins

Natives are tough plants, specialized for particular locales. Even if you have a garden full of nonnatives, there's an important reason to consider natives: they are hosts for some of Colorado's most beautiful butterflies.

One couple moved into a mountain cabin only to discover that it changed their lives. Renovating a 1940s cabin was a labor of love. With it came a simpler and, they say, better way of life.

John Brocklehurst's gardens lie at 8,700 feet in a windswept valley. As a transplanted English gardener, John has employed his vast knowledge in coaxing plants to flourish in difficult conditions.

■ Era of Gentility: Victorians

These lovely, feminine houses evoke lilacs and lace, but many are sadly out of date or in need of repair. One family decided to expand and embellish upon a sturdy home in need of an update. In doing so, they passed the code in a historic district.

Lilacs, tall bearded irises, and hardy roses have a place in Colorado gardens. Most were brought out west by turn-of-the-century transplants, and several have survived. You'll find old-fashioned French lilacs, irises, and Harison's yellow roses on nineteenth-century farmsteads.

CONTENTS

Although the West capitalizes on its rough-and-tumble image, Colorado once scorned it and embraced gentility in the early part of the twentieth century. The most admired culture was England's, and a Tudor-style home was envied by all.

On the University of Colorado–Boulder campus, a Shakespearean garden accompanies the Colorado Shakespeare Festival each summer. Although reminders of Elizabethan days, some old-fashioned flowers, such as the Johnny-jump-ups and violets, naturally acclimated to Colorado's climate.

◼ ORDINARY COMFORT: BUNGALOWS AND COTTAGES

Victoriana may evoke femininity, but the craftsman bungalow is strictly masculine. A lodge by the lake filled with comfortable overstuffed furniture remains inviting. Bungalows were shipped out west by railroad, and today their popularity is soaring.

After summer's flowers have faded and disappeared, conifers claim the Colorado landscape. We take them for granted, but conifers define our scenery. It's only when we get to know them that we appreciate their resilient beauty.

You can't beat a cottage for comfortable, cozy, and romantic living. Contemporary living in a small space can be just as inviting today as it was in 1906.

The exuberance of a cottage garden is wildly popular today. Cheerful and informal, a cottage garden delights us with a profusion of blooms and a variety of shapes and colors.

■ ATOMIC-AGE CLASSICS: COLORADO MODERNISM

In the 1950s and 1960s, strong, bold designs incorporated simple geometric features. Clean, pure lines appealed to those who rejected fussy detail or ornamentation. Eventually, this modern look became as cloying as the heavy-handed style it was meant to replace. But good modern design does exist and remains beautiful still.

An ancient art in China and Europe, rock gardening is a recent addition to American horticulture. In Colorado, alpine rock gardens have become a passion in the study of both alpine plants and the ecology that shelters them.

■ CREATIVE SOLUTIONS: HOMES AND GARDENS OF THE FUTURE

A professor of architecture has set about to build her dream home. Recycled, energy-wise, easy to maintain—this may be the home of the future. In this comfortable and casual dwelling, the building materials are surprisingly creative.

Xeric means "dry" in Greek. In English, it simply refers to the wise use of water. The concept has caught on with environmentalists, water conservators, low-maintenance gardeners, and landscape architects.

At the foot of a bluff in Trinidad, Colorado, Jennifer Green's adobe house is near completion, a new house in a region that has birthed adobe homes for more than one hundred years. Using her own hands, the petite third-grade teacher shaped, hoisted, and placed brick after brick.

When I first met with the original writers at Front Range Living nearly three years ago, most of us had arrived from the world of Colorado newspapers. All of us had experience covering the daily stories of everyday life and we wanted to continue to do so—but in a different arena with a new slant. Together we hammered out the areas that we believed were of compelling interest to readers. One was the cultural world of history, design, and architecture. The other was the natural world, whether cultivated in gardens or visited on a mountainside.

We pooled our ideas and came up with a philosophy for covering the immense and spectacular terrain of Colorado. And while there are magazines devoted to environmental concerns and books devoted to extreme sports, we imagined chapters more personal, almost like a diary.

"Animals," said Dianne Zuckerman, who has always championed the feathered and furred. For this former theater critic for newspapers and magazines, the natural world is a tooth-and-claw stage, full of crises and struggles, winners and losers.

"Leisure and fun, too," said Beth Krodel, who loves to soak in a hot springs after a day of hiking. Following a stint as a foreign correspondent in the Middle East, Beth is content to find adventure closer to home.

"Learning about the rocks, plants, and land formations," was my response. No one can overlook our spectacular rocks, but I wanted to write about the smaller worlds, too—the delicate pasque flower with petals as thin as tissue, the migration of butterflies in mid-July, and the call of birds that flock around Barr Lake.

We would take our readers on journeys into our wide-open spaces and ask questions that any ordinary person might ask. And then we would report back. Not one of us is a scientist or an Olympic athlete. We would search for outdoor experiences that anyone would enjoy. And in most cases, these would be trips on which you could take a child, mother, neighbor, or friend.

When Carol Ward and I sat down to discuss how best to cover antiques in Colorado, we came with similar perspectives. We wanted to introduce our readers to the joys—and caveats—of collecting. Whether you crave the rustic lodge look or the frills of Victoriana, we would search for solid information. "Old World elegance," Carol, who loves the country styles of Europe, said, "History as it is handed down in objects and places or a prized possession that tells a story." Together we have searched for stories that cover Colorado uniquely: our love for all things Western, casual interiors that mix the old with the new, appreciation of workmanship and craft, glassware, jewelry styles, or silver serving utensils that never will be made again.

In doing so, we talked to dealers who have become experts in their fields and to collectors who have amassed a valuable group, or, more often, simply indulged in an affordable passion. Antiques are linked to our cultural history and reveal the abrupt changes in our homes, children's playthings, dining habits, entertainment, and fashion.

If antique stories divulge the small details of the past, homes and gardens tell volumes. Houses from previous generations reveal not only the strata of the wealthy and working classes, but also the dominant art of the day: arts and crafts, English Tudor, Spanish adobe, Victorian neo-Gothic. Gardens, too, are linked to the buildings they surround, like petticoats enhancing the prima ballerina. Colorado contains the comfortably worn and the cutting-edge. Heidi Anderson and I searched for old and new, grand and modest, historical and modern. Where she found recycled, renewable, revamped architecture, I found familiarity in bungalows, Victorians, and modernist design.

Gardening brings a history through the decades as well. Before drought gripped Colorado, scientists voiced concern that we were stretching our water supplies. Living in a semiarid climate, coupled with the influx of new residents, makes water conservation a hot topic for gardeners. The answer to wise planting may be in native plants that predate any people at all. Or, perhaps the old-fashioned plants that have survived adverse conditions over many decades will shape our landscape. Then, there are the newer imported plants that are drought-resistant in other climes and have successfully adapted to our own. We interviewed successful amateurs and seasoned professionals—each devoted to an informal laboratory—the garden.

Our readership grew slowly but surely. The Internet has become an effective way to provide low cost information to millions of readers—to have a personal relationship with those readers and act quickly, correct errors, and build archives of value. For a magazine, the Internet becomes an incubator. What do your readers choose? How can writers tailor their stories to readers' needs? Whether cooking fresh produce from the farmers markets or learning about growing culinary herbs, we were able to discover which stories were most popular. We followed those interests and continue to do so.

A few readers asked if we would consider collecting stories in book form. Computers, they suggested, were fine for working and researching, but not comfortable to curl up with on a cold winter night. Readers, they told us, like books, too. Now we have partnered with Fulcrum Publishing in Golden, who has guided us in the first of an extended series. We'll begin with guides to the Colorado outdoors, antiques, and homes and gardens, with more to come in the future. The old and new have conjoined. And whether you love the Internet, or prefer books, Front Range Living will give you the best of both worlds.

Paper or cyberspace—it still comes down to words and whether they engage, enlighten, or entertain us. New communications technologies alter those they push aside, but the old are remarkably resilient. The Internet won't do away with books. In fact, the two have become the newest of best friends. Front Range Living will provide an ongoing source of Colorado experiences for our readers. But when the day ends, and you want to slip under bedcovers with a cup of tea and a good book, we'll be available as a bedside companion, too.

—Niki Hayden, Editor
Front Range Living

Colorado's architectural heritage isn't terribly old, unless you count Mesa Verde, which classifies as ancient. Compared to the East Coast, we're upstarts, products of the late nineteenth century. Today, Colorado is filled with turn-of-the-century homes that may not be old enough to be considered treasures, but are mature enough to need help. Many of us are grappling with renewing a Victorian, expanding a bungalow, downsizing to a cottage, or considering how best to remodel a 1950s tract home.

But how to approach such daunting tasks? Fortunately, we have remarkable resources all around. If you'd like to understand your old house better, get in touch with the closest local historic society. Most will have lists of architects and builders who specialize in a house of your era. Look for antique dealers who carry period artifacts that might relate to your home. And, for a close glimpse of sensitive updating, search for historic homes open to the public.

Colorado Preservation, Inc. (www.coloradopreservation.org), is a good place to start. But you'll also find Historic Denver (www.historicdenver.org) and Historic Boulder (www.historicboulder.org) to be of great help, too.

Got a 1950s home that needs help? Until recently, these homes were simply looked upon as fodder for pop-ups. No more. They have a clout all their own now that modernism is prized. Your tract house may not be old enough to be considered historical, but there are plenty of shops that sell original stuff from the 1950s as well as reproductions. From architectural artifacts to furniture, there's more available to choose from than ever before.

If you're building a new home, consider some of the products that use recycled materials. University of Colorado architecture professor Julee Herdt is on the forefront of developing building supplies for houses that will lead to environmental and financial savings in new homes. Linoleum, structural insulated panels, and energy-saving hot-water systems—these old and new products are either on the market now or will be soon.

Earth-based buildings, such as adobe and rammed earth, are making a new appearance as well. Although earth houses are not widespread, new adobe homes have been built in Trinidad, Cortez, and Boulder.

Of course, every house needs a garden. Even the smallest home with a sidewalk rather than a yard can be made stunning by including a patio garden. Vegetables, herbs, flowers, and showy foliage plants can share space in pots.

New homes often come with tiny yards. That makes an ideal landscape for rock and cottage gardens. Colorado is a prime spot for rock gardening, and the Denver Botanic Gardens, with its stunning rock gardens, is testimony to that. You'll find regional rock-garden societies that will help you get started. And cottage gardens are the perfect partner for bungalows.

For those who yearn for an old-fashioned perennial garden, there is hope. Not all such traditional gardens are water guzzlers. Lilacs, bearded irises, and hardy roses are just a few old-timer perennials that are drought-resistant, appropriate for a Victorian home, and beautiful. These three garden stalwarts are so water thrifty that you'll often find them listed as water-wise plants for those looking to conserve.

In times of drought and water restrictions, tough native plants and sturdy drought-resistant xeric gardens come to the rescue. Colorado's is a semi-arid landscape, so natives are well-adapted. Imported drought-resistant beauties are elegant, too. Our environment is different from the East and West Coasts, but capable of extraordinary gardens. Look into classes at the Denver Botanic Gardens (www.botanicgardens.org), and consider the master gardener classes at your county's Colorado State University Cooperative Extension office to learn from the experts.

Visit important gardens in Colorado to see what grows well here: the Denver Botanic Gardens for rock gardens, prairie gardens, annuals, and perennials; the Jefferson County Jail (yes, unusual—but spectacular) for roses; the Betty Ford Alpine Gardens in Vail (www.bettyfordalpinegardens.org) for alpines and natives.

The Garden Conservancy tours (www.gardenconservancy.org) for home gardens can't be beat. Each year they focus on one or two cities to showcase some of the best home gardens. In the past, Denver and Colorado Springs have been chosen. There are plenty of local garden tours, too; these are usually sponsored by local charities. Check your local garden centers for listings of these informal tours.

In Colorado, we've been fortunate that many of our cities never experienced the dreary urban renewal that razed entire neighborhoods elsewhere. We have been able to keep our Victorians, bungalows, cottages, and ranch houses. Our cities are teeming with outstanding masonry and historic districts. More than ever, homeowners are renovating their historic homes with an eye toward preserving rather than destroying the original. The result is a wonderful display of history along our city streets.

So consider visiting some fine examples of historic homes: Hoverhome in Longmont, the Baca House and Bloom Mansion in Trinidad, the Boettcher Mansion in Golden, Rosemount in Pueblo, the Molly Brown House or Byers-Evans House in Denver, the Meeker Home in Greeley, the Arnett-Fullen House in Boulder. From adobe to Victorian to arts and crafts, these homes have preserved styles that represent colorful decades in Colorado. All are open to the public and will take you back in time.

RUSTIC GEMS:

Colorado Cabins

One example is milkweed *(Asclepias tuberosa terminalis),* the host plant for monarch butterflies. Monarch caterpillars feast on the leaves of the milkweed, which contain a strong poison. They then store a form of that poison, and once they change into butterflies, birds won't eat them. This relationship is so ancient that without milkweed, there would be no monarch butterflies.

Milkweed is rarely grown as a landscape plant, but as the habitat for this plant dwindles, so does the number of monarch butterflies.

Chokecherry (*Padus virginiana* spp.) is the host for the tiger swallowtail butterfly. Where you find a patch of native blue-purple tall beard-tongue penstemons *(Penstemon virgatus),* you're sure to find a colony of hummingbirds. Each of these plants can be grown in home gardens.

HOW TO GET STARTED

Many gardeners would love to incorporate natives into their home landscapes but don't know where to find them or how to grow them. There's no single solution to every plant.

Many drought-tolerant plants, like the spotted gayfeather *(Liatris punctata),* may develop long taproots to adapt to dry conditions as does the butterfly milkweed *(A. tuberosa).* Neither will survive as a transplant from the wild.

Most drought-tolerant natives develop long taproots that will snap off if you try to dig them up. A better approach is to try growing them from seed. Sometimes the seed can be broadcast on soil. Most can be grown from seed in a small pot and transplanted when a few inches high. Either way, the delicate taproot will remain intact.

The perils of transplanting make it foolish to collect any plant from the wild. Most established plants simply won't transplant at all. Instead, Kathy offers a few suggestions to get you started with nearly foolproof plants for the Front Range.

First, decide how much space in your yard you want to allot to natives. Consider microclimates. Maybe the plants you choose need a southeastern exposure. Or, perhaps a fence shades a portion of your yard. The small differences in your yard replicate the microclimates in Colorado, whether it's the shaded north side of a mountain or the sunny south slope of a valley.

Get a soil analysis to find out what nutrients are in your soil. Your county agricultural extension office should be able to help you with instructions on taking a sample of your soil, which you can then take to them for analysis.

Decide how groomed you want your lawn to be. Kathy chose buffalo and blue grama grasses for her lawn: "They only need about four mowings a year. That's only because occasionally I want to tidy the lawn up a bit," she says. If you like the length of these grasses, you don't need to mow them at all.

Then she picked out a few terrific natives as the backbone of her garden, mostly shrubs. Two mountain mahogany shrubs went in: *Cercocarpus montanus* and a *C. ledifolius*. She says *C. ledifolius* is native to northwest Colorado, so go with the *C. montanus* if you live elsewhere.

For ground covers, consider *Mahonia repens,* or Oregon grape, as a low-growing shrub. You can't beat pussytoes *(Antennaria parvifolia),* with its matted silvery leaves, to fill in the crevices of a rock walkway.

Winecups *(Callirhoe involucrata),* a ground cover with purple-cupped flowers that arch above wiry, hairy stems, is impervious to drought. It spreads easily along a blistering sidewalk where most plants shrivel.

A striking native ornamental grass is little bluestem *(Schizachyrium scoparium).*

Spotted gayfeather *(Liatris punctata)* is a favorite nectar source for butterflies.

Add blanket flower *(Gaillardia aristata)* for a yellowish-orange burst of color. Of course, all of these grow best in the plains and foothills. They like dry, alkaline soil with bright sun. And most can be found in Colorado nurseries.

Native grasses are generally drought tolerant, but do require a good match between soil and plant.

When you shop at a nursery or from a catalog, be sure to use the Latin name of the plant. Native plants are notorious for sharing look-alike popular names so confusing to the everyday gardener (for example, several native plants are called "butterfly plant"). Kathy planted a hackberry tree (the netleaf hackberry is a native), and only after it languished in her garden did she discover that it was a hackberry native to the Midwest *(Celtis occidentalis).*

Consider Your Terrain

Finally, consider your watering schedule. Kathy watered twice a week in the spring when she first planted. (Plants require more water in the beginning to establish an extensive root system.) Of course, that may not be necessary if there's sufficient rainfall. Many native plants are accustomed to spring snow runoff, especially in the foothills. By summer, she began tapering off her waterings. Once established, her plants required little care and less water.

It is difficult to recommend trees that will thrive. The typical native, such as the cottonwood, grows by a stream with its roots deeply extended into the water. It's not a drought-tolerant tree. This is true for most of the Great Plains, where trees evolved to flourish near streams. After all, the Colorado prairie was once covered with grasses and wildflowers.

In the mountains, where water runs downhill alongside its roots, you'll find aspen trees thriving. Aspens prefer mountain temperatures and hilly terrain to

A white evening primrose *(Oenothera caespitosa)* likes a hot, dry garden and blooms in the early evening.

having their roots sit in water on flat land. Neither cotton-woods nor aspen will grow spectacularly well without extensive irrigation.

Other gardeners coax ponderosa pine and blue spruce at lower altitudes. A blue spruce requires more water than a ponderosa pine, the latter of which is most comfortable set apart from lawns. Too much lawn watering will stress the pine's roots and it will become fragile.

There is one tried-and-true native tree that will thrive. Although you'll find it next to cottonwoods along creek sides, it has adapted to grow on rocky, dry mountainsides: the netleaf hackberry *(Celtis reticulata)*. Another bonus— it's the host for a native Colorado butterfly.

A Guide for Natives

Here's a guide to natives that will thrive according to their preferred environment in Colorado:

MOUNTAINS

Trees: ponderosa pine *(Pinus ponderosa);* aspen *(Populus tremuloides);* blue spruce *(Picea pungens).*

Perennial flowers: Rocky Mountain penstemon *(Penstemon strictus);* Rocky Mountain iris *(Iris missouriensis).*

Shrubs: red-berried elder *(Sambucus microbotrys);* shrubby cinquefoil *(Pentaphylloides floribunda);* wild rose *(Rosa woodsii).*

FOOTHILLS

Tree: netleaf hackberry *(Celtis reticulata).*

Shrubs: Boulder raspberry *(Oreobatus deliciosus);* false indigo, also known as leadplant *(Amorpha fruticosa).*

Perennial flowers: wild geranium *(Geranium caespitosum);* wild bergamot, also known as wild bee balm *(Monarda fistulosa);* spiderwort *(Tradescantia occidentalis);* firecracker penstemon *(Penstemon pinifolius).* These plants require more water than those from the dry plains, so if you are close to but not a part of the foothills, consider your garden to be in the plains environment.

PLAINS

Trees: Consider the scrub oak, also called Gambel oak *(Quercus gambelii)* for dry slopes. If you live in the south or southwest of Colorado, take a look at the piñon pine *(Pinus edulis).*

Shrubs: antelope bitterbush *(Purshia tridentata);* rabbitbrush *(Chryso-thamnus nauseosus);* narrow-leaf Great yucca *(Yucca glauca).*

Perennial flowers: yellow stemless evening primrose *(Oenothera howardii);* wild verbena *(Glandularia bipinnatifida);* spotted gayfeather *(Liatris punctata);* scarlet globe mallow *(Sphaeralcea coccinea).*

HOW TO CULTIVATE A BUTTERFLY GARDEN: AN INTERVIEW WITH GEORGE BRINKMANN

George Brinkmann is a native landscape and habitat restoration consultant. He's the retired horticulturist from the Butterfly Pavilion in Westminster and a teacher and staff horticulturist at the Denver Botanic Gardens. Colorado is home to 250 species of butterflies, more than anywhere else in North America. On any July day, if you hike on Mount Evans, you'll see a variety of native butterflies.

Front Range Living (FRL): How do you set about to plant a butterfly garden, and is that related to other insects as well?

George Brinkmann (GB): I think they are very interrelated. You need three elements. You need host plants that the butterflies feed on. You also need nectar sources and shelter.

To broaden that to a habitat garden, we are talking about other insects—pollinators like honeybees, ladybird beetles, and different kinds of flies. Your aim is to get a mix of critters that balance themselves. They all need nectar sources.

A wide range of yarrows (*Achillea* spp.) makes a significant contribution to the native garden.

Rabbitbrush is excellent, mint and thyme are pollen or nectar sources and easy to grow in this Rocky Mountain area. Incorporate these into your landscape and they'll feed a number of insects. I have rabbitbrush at the pavilion. It blooms in late summer and must have over one hundred honeybees on it.

FRL: How do you go about choosing plants?

GB: First, you need to plant native material. One thing you need to understand is the life cycle of the butterfly. The eggs are laid only on a host plant. The young caterpillars will only eat on a specific plant before they change into a chrysalis, the pupa stage, and then to a butterfly. Each species of butterfly has its own plant that it survives on.

For the black swallowtail, it's dill or parsley. Many skippers (native prairie flies) feed on grasses on the prairie; the variegated fritillary is a native and feeds on blue flax. The most common is the painted lady, and it feeds on thistle. If you eliminate the plant, you eliminate that species. For example, if you don't have milkweed, you won't have monarchs. Grow milkweed, *Asclepias tuberosa*, called butterfly weed, or *Asclepias incarnata*. Both grow well in Colorado and are perennials. *Incarnata* grows where it's wet. Grow chokecherry, the host plant for the tiger swallowtail, the largest butterfly in Colorado.

FRL: How would you go about designing such a garden?

GB: Besides natives, you can also use cultivars or hybrids in garden design. You need to have plants that grow in a specific environment. For example, if you have an area that is hot and dry, then you need plants that thrive: cactus, prickly pear, penstemon—both native or hybrid.

Since you plant annuals in the spring, I'd pick the best for nectar source, and zinnia is the best. I always say, "Plant them and they will come." So if you plant zinnias, you'll get butterflies and bees. Another annual is verbena; there's a particular variety called 'Homestead Purple' that's good. But there are many others, too. Some are annuals; some are perennials. One exceptional verbena is *bonariensis.* It grows two to three feet tall and reseeds itself. Another annual is the Mexican sunflower, *Tithonia rotundifolia.* All these are available in garden centers.

Winecups *(Callirhoe involucrata)* is a drought-tolerant ground cover that grows well in clay soil, a hardy native that has adapted to many Colorado landscapes.

You'd be surprised at how much habitat for butterflies we're losing every day. You don't attract butterflies with bluegrass, junipers, or crushed rocks, and yet they are so extensively used.

FRL: Do butterflies also need water, or boggy areas?

GB: Yes, sometimes you'll see butterflies clustered on the ground when you're hiking. That's called puddling. They're getting salt and moisture from mud. They'll suck the minerals like calcium from the ground, which they need.

Fireflies only exist in bog areas. We have natural bog areas all over Colorado. Roxborough State Park is one; Chatfield Arboretum is another. These are natural wetlands and we need to preserve these areas. In the metropolitan area of Denver there are a number of small bog areas.

FRL: How would you design a garden for spring, summer, and fall?

GB: The spring bloomers would be viburnum, spiraeas, lilacs—the flowering shrubs. Then by summer some of the buddleias, the butterfly bush, will bloom, although many of those are late summer. Then in the summer you have your annuals, like zinnia, and perennials. Then blue mist spiraea, which is not a real spiraea, is good for late summer. It also attracts bees. In the fall, sedum, such as dragon's blood, draws insects—also milkweed and rudbeckia. It's not the size of the garden that's important, but the plant material. You don't have to have a big garden; it could even be a flower box on your patio.

FRL: What about people who don't want to attract wasps or bees?

GB: Some people don't like wasps or bees, but without these pollinators, you would not have squash, cucumbers, tomatoes, apples, or any fruits. To have pollinators, you have to grow without insecticides. What I've discovered at the Butterfly Pavilion, with no toxic elements, is that nature has balanced itself. I have no injuries with insects. If you have insects on your plants that you don't want, just prune off the affected portions or use water to hose off the aphids. Use the least toxic control that you can.

I'm seventy years old, so I came from a whole different way of growing plants. I worked in a greenhouse, and we used the most toxic ingredients known to man, derived from nerve gases. We got tremendous effects for a while. Then insects became immune to that. Plus, from a medical standpoint, it's dangerous. I had a mask that leaked one time and I spent a night in the hospital. I'm so relieved to get away from that.

FRL: What are the best ways to provide shelter?

GB: To attract butterflies and birds, you need trees and shrubs like the serviceberry bush or a crab apple tree. You need a windbreak like a big rock, because when a butterfly opens its wings it's soaking up solar energy. Big slabs of rocks on the top of a berm give you pockets for the butterflies to hide in, and you may have three generations over the summer.

For the butterflies, which lay eggs in the fall that in turn live throughout the winter, the chrysalis will be attached to the bottom of a rock. The mourning cloak butterfly winters as an adult; those are the first you'll see in the spring in the canyons above Boulder. That's a native butterfly. They can winter over in cold temperatures.

The message is to restore habitat, and you can do that in a small way in your yard. Collectively, if everyone cooperated, that would be a big impact.

RESOURCES

■ GARDEN CENTERS

The Flower Bin, 1805 Nelson Road, Longmont, 80501; 303-772-3454. Natives and drought-tolerant ornamentals.

Fort Collins Nursery, 2121 East Mulberry Street, Fort Collins, 80524; 970-482-1984; www.fortcollinsnursery.com. Natives and drought-tolerant ornamentals.

■ MAIL-ORDER NURSERIES

High Country Gardens (Santa Fe Greenhouses), 2902 Rufina Street, Santa Fe, New Mexico 87505; 800-925-9387; www.highcountrygardens.com. Carries many ornamental, drought-tolerant plants, with some natives.

Sunscapes Rare Plant Nursery, 330 Carlile Avenue, Pueblo, 81004; 719-546-0047; www.sunscapes.net. Rock-garden plants, smaller dwarf plants, alpines, mostly dryland rockeries, including the penstemon family. Also xeric landscaping. Mostly catalog sales; visits by appointment only.

■ RECOMMENDED READING

Grow Native: Landscaping with Native and Apt Plants of the Rocky Mountains by S. Huddleston
and M. Hussey (Fulcrum Publishing, 1998).

Native Plants for High-Elevation Western Gardens by Janice Busco and Nancy R. Morin
(Fulcrum Publishing, 2003, in partnership with The Arboretum at Flagstaff).

■ SEED COMPANIES

Alplains, P.O. Box 489, Kiowa, 80117; 303-621-2247. Seeds for unusual alpine plants; desert to
alpine. Catalog upon request for a small fee. Specializes in penstemon, lilium, dianthus, cacti;
seven hundred species of seeds.

Plants of the Southwest, 3095 Agua Fria Road, Santa Fe, New Mexico 87107; 800-788-7333;
www.plantsofthesouthwest.com.

Rocky Mountain Rare Plants, 1706 Deerpath Road, Franktown, 80116; e-mail: staff@rmrp.com;
www.rmrp.com. Specializes in seeds for alpine plants.

Western Native Seed, P.O. Box 188, Coaldale, 81222; 719-942-3935; www.westernnativeseed.com.
Wide variety of wildflowers.

■ WEBSITE

Colorado Native Plant Society, P.O. Box 200, Fort Collins, 80522; www.conps.org. Site lists
appropriate native plants for landscaping as well as links to other resource sites.

■ THE COLORADO MOUNTAIN CABIN: A RETREAT BECOMES A WAY OF LIFE

by NIKI HAYDEN

Books and magazines tell us stories about how a house has changed a life. Usually it's a villa in Italy, or an apartment in Paris. A seaside beach house soothes the soul, or a midwestern farm evokes nostalgia. Homes have the power to create memories. Do they also have the power to transform lives? Perhaps they do.

For Ted Warren, a primitive cabin—not a villa or penthouse—changed his life forever. The mountain cabin where Ted and Peggy Warren live was to be a summer place, a studio where they could draw and paint. Built in the 1940s, the handsome one-room cabin came with electricity but no running water. A large fireplace warmed bitter nights, but there was no bathroom, no bedroom, no kitchen cabinets.

The Warren cabin is surrounded by aspen trees and raised beds of lettuces, columbine hybrids, and Iceland poppies.

Peggy thought having a mountain cabin would offer a quiet getaway from the summer heat of their Dallas home. They could rough it on a vacation. She never intended to spend more than a month or two in such primitive conditions, so they bought the only cabin for sale in a small mountain community. That was eleven years ago when Ted was fifty-eight.

"I heard Ted on the phone suggesting that he was going to sell the business in Dallas and live here. He didn't even go back to Dallas to close the office. I did that," Peggy says. "Forty years of belongings were moved into a one-room cabin. It came as a shock. He was good at making money and I was good at spending it." The Warrens sold nearly everything they owned, reserving some rustic western furniture from their east Texas ranch to fill the Colorado cabin.

Making a Cabin a Home

Over the last decade, the Warren cabin has changed in amenities, but not in spirit. It remains true to its origins: rough logs with a chink of cement and horsehair surrounding a rock fireplace of gathered stones. The lines are simple and basic, serviceable and sturdy. But now it does have a well, a septic tank, and two bathrooms. There's a painting studio for Peggy and one for Ted. A bedroom has been added and the kitchen includes cabinets. But the

Ted and Peggy kept a few pieces of rustic Western furniture, cowboy hats, paintings, and photographs for their 1940s cabin.

cabin's original room is still the main living area, serving as living room, dining room, and kitchen. All together, the home is now about 1,200 square feet.

With walls lined in cowboy hats, family photos, and paintings, the furnishings are rustic and personal. Bright red leather couches covered with colorful woven blankets face the rock fireplace, and striking rugs hug the wood floors. Two friendly beagles loll on one of the couches. Outside, the cabin is nestled among aspen trees and raised beds of columbines, strawberries, lettuces, and Iceland poppies.

Ted gleaned both a knowledge of cabin construction and an understanding of its history as he renovated. As simple as the western log cabin may be, he says it's not an easy construction. "I have a lot of admiration for those who built these cabins. Trying to get the logs straight, and just lifting them is difficult. The effort that goes into setting them perfectly flat," he says with a shake of his head. "There are still enough people in the mountains who've built log cabins; you can still do it the old way."

Using Time-Honored Techniques

Mountain cabins come with unique characteristics. They can be cold, dark, and perched on shaky foundations. Ted did his best to alter all three conditions. The bedroom was built to match the original cabin as closely as possible, with trees hand-shaved and carefully measured. The chink that fills in gaps between logs was modernized. The cement and horsehair mixture isn't worth replicating—it's too rigid and fragile. Now carpenters use a vinyl chink, which will stretch and give, unlike the old.

Ted's cabin carpenters approached a felled tree with time-honored techniques and modern creativity. Tree trunks were split in half and insulation squeezed between. And a new roof was built on top of the old, with insulation sandwiched between them.

Open shelves, simple appliances, and old-fashioned cabin charm was worth preserving.

Every new technique to renovate cabins is aimed at keeping precious heat in and a howling winter wind out. "You can always tell if a cabin roof has been insulated, just by the thickness of the roof," Ted says. Skylights were cut into the roofs in every room, and the light that filters in relieves the original darkness of a log interior.

Cabins depart from conventional construction. You won't find many mountain cabins built with basements. The ground is too rocky, and, in the Warrens' case, the water table too high. Down the road a bit, a backhoe dutifully dug a foundation cellar, and Ted says more rocks were extracted from the hole than could have fit back in. Ted and Peggy's 1940s cabin is set on concrete piers—quite a feat in any decade. The gap that remained between house and ground has since been filled in with concrete.

The two painting studios depart from the cabin's interior with white walls and large windows.

Although Ted's not a stickler for historical accuracy, he loves to keep the continuity of design in his small space. Hunting down places to buy wood that matched his home and ambitions paid off. He discovered local sawmills and bought rough-sawn wood. "Well, it shrinks," he says as a warning. So he would allow it to dry for six months before building with it. Working with rough-cut wood, shaving the bark off trees with a two-handed saw, and mixing chink were specialty crafts he discovered that several of his neighbors had mastered.

The new logs are stained with brown and red to match the original dark brown logs. Then they are oiled every three years. "Building log cabins, and all that goes into it—well, that's a local lore in mountain towns," Ted says. "The whole thing was an athletic exercise."

The Warrens revamped a few amenities: up-to-date electrical wiring and a well, which was sunk 425 feet deep for $12,000. Propane heaters radiate warmth. In their mountain town, not all their neighbors have running water, but all have electricity. Some of the cabins around Ted and Peggy are more than a hundred years old and haven't changed much in the last century. Few were meant for winter living. But times have changed in mountain towns. In the last ten years, residents, like Peggy and Ted, have decided to live there year-round, winterizing their summer homes. "It takes three months to do anything," coincidentally, the length of summer, Ted warns, no matter how small or insignificant.

Still, he wouldn't have it any other way. In the last ten years, Ted has bought and fixed up other cabins, Peggy has opened and sold a bookstore, bagel and coffee shop, and ice-cream parlor. They've met everyone in their valley, worked on civic projects, and learned to live through tough winters.

Ten years ago, Ted estimates that only thirty people lived in the community year-round—several were hardy widows who knew how to live without running water or indoor bathrooms, he says. Today, he estimates the population to be closer to 130, and newcomers want an easier lifestyle. They learn to accommodate themselves to cold winters, snowy roads, and long drives—or they leave. Ted says he never feels trapped in mid-winter. "I wasn't much of a traveler anyway. And it's still nice here in the winter. Everybody who

lives here is trying to escape from something. For me it was a retreat. We lived in downtown Dallas. We always worked in the city and went to the country on the weekends."

Peggy loves the cabin, too—but not all the time. She keeps a small apartment in the city and meets friends for dinner and the theater. "I'm a people person," she says, "and I love the bustle of the city." But as to previous homes and furnishings— "We sold all that," Ted says with a wave of his hand, "and wanted to live a simpler life."

Nestled behind aspen trees, the Warren cabin has become a permanent retreat.

RESOURCES

■ MUSEUMS

Baca House, Bloom Mansion, and Pioneer Museum, 300 East Main Street, Trinidad, 81082;

719-846-7217; www.coloradohistory.org/hist_sites/trinidad/bacahouse.htm.

Buffalo Bill Cody Memorial Museum and Grave, 987-1/2 Lookout Mountain Road, Golden,

80401; 303-526-0747; www.buffalobill.org.

Colorado History Museum, 1300 Broadway, Denver, 80203; 303-866-3682;

www.coloradohistory.org.

Colorado Springs Fine Arts Center, 30 West Dale Street, Colorado Springs, 80903;

719-634-5581; www.csfineartscenter.org. Hispanic and Pueblo collections as well as

traditional western art.

Hiwan Homestead Museum, 4208 South Timbervale Drive, Evergreen, 80439; 303-674-6262;

http://ww2.co.jefferson.co.us/ext/dpt/comm_res/openspac/hiwan.htm. A nineteenth-century

log home furnished in the western style of the 1920s and 1930s.

Pro Rodeo Hall of Fame, 101 Pro Rodeo Drive, Colorado Springs, 80919; 719-593-8840;

www.prorodeo.com.

■ RUSTIC AND MOUNTAIN FURNITURE

Little Bear Antiques & Uniques, 415 South Spring Street, Aspen, 81611; 970-925-3705.

Shepton's Antiques, 389 South Broadway, Denver, 80209; 303-777-5115.

Rustic teak, pine, architectural.

Ski Country Antiques, 114 Homestead Road, Evergreen, 80439; 303-674-4666.

■ WESTERN FURNITURE AND ACCESSORIES

Antique Accents, 155 Main Street, Minturn, 81645; 970-827-9070. Antiques and memorabilia.

Cowboy Classics; e-mail: cowgirl1919@aol.com; www.t-m-cowboyclassics.com. Tom and Maril

Bice make and sell western furniture from their home in Longmont and sell it over the Internet.

Cry Baby Ranch, 1422 Larimer Street, Denver, 80202; 303-623-3979; www.crybabyranch.com. Large selection of western collectibles, clothing, home decor.

Crystal Farm, 18 Antelope Road, Redstone, 81623; 970-963-2350; www.crystalfarm.com. Antler furniture and lighting.

Frontier Gallery (Antique Exchange), 1500 South Broadway, Denver, 80210; 303-733-4200. Memorabilia.

Gallagher Collection, 1298 South Broadway, Denver, 80201, in the Antique Guild; 303-756-5821. Books only.

High Country Furniture & Gallery, Inc. 68 Ninth Street, Steamboat Springs, 80487; 970-879-2670.

Into the West, 807 Lincoln Avenue, Steamboat Springs, 80487; 970-879-8377.

Kemo Sabe, 434 East Cooper Avenue, Aspen, 81611; 970-925-7878. Western hats, boots, home furnishings.

Left-Hand Trading Company, 401 Main Street, Lyons, 80540; 303-823-6311; www.lefthandtradingcompany.com. Western room filled with antique furniture, accessories, books, jewelry.

Ruxton's Trading Post, 22 Ruxton Avenue, Manitou Springs, 80829; 719-635-0588; www.oldwestantiques.com. Wide range of western items; also information on the Pikes Peak Western Show.

Telluride Antique Market, 324 West Colorado Avenue, Telluride, 81435; 970-728-4323. Western memorabilia.

Western Shop, 807 Manitou Avenue, Manitou Springs, 80829; 719-685-5026. Western clothing.

White Hart Gallery, 843 Lincoln Avenue, Steamboat Springs, 80487; 970-879-1015.

■ AGAINST THE ODDS: GARDENING IN COLORADO'S HIGH COUNTRY

by NIKI HAYDEN

John Brocklehurst has never taken his garden for granted. In a windswept valley 8,700 feet in elevation, winter temperatures drop to twenty below zero. Summer rockets to ninety degrees. John has tended this garden for fourteen years, learning with each season how to garden at high altitude in Colorado.

John's wife, Willi, relaxes in a swing next to a swollen river. Hummingbirds zip and dart from feeder to feeder. To the uninformed, it's a scene that defies drought or fire, although both are threatening his community. "Come into the garden," he invites a neighbor walking her dog. The garden is to be savored and, as if in a sympathetic gesture, blooms profusely.

Anyone who has tended a high-altitude garden can list the woes aside from fire and drought: rocky soil, hailstorms, bitter cold winds, unpredictable frosts. To undertake a garden as lavish as the Brocklehursts' requires knowledge and skill. John has both. He's a transplanted English horticulturist trained at the Royal Agriculture College. Willi is an American who spent part of her childhood in England. They retired to a mountain cabin where John indulges his passion for plants in one of the most daunting environments. Out of a fierce climate, he has coaxed a garden with an individual stamp that also imparts a sense of harmony. Nothing is out of place.

Columbines, ferns, and Iceland poppies mix together in John Brocklehurst's mountain woodland garden.

21

John's move to Colorado was sparked by the nineteenth-century memoir of fellow Brit, Isabella Bird. *A Lady's Life in the Rocky Mountains* (London: John Murray, 1879; University of Oklahoma Press, 1999) inspired him to follow her footsteps. "I drove out on an exploratory trip to Estes Park in 1977," he says, and ended up looking for work in Colorado. Eventually, he was "mowing those bloody highway medians—it was dreadful."

John couldn't resist a visual pun when he added a new bed of flowers.

In time, he designed several municipal Colorado gardens and mastered the rigors of Colorado soils and climate. Along the way, John applied his knowledge of gardening to a one-third-acre plot surrounding the mountain cabin that he and Willi call home. Willi is not a gardener herself, but appreciates the sitting area under a tree, afternoon tea at a table under an umbrella by the side of the river, and a hammock slung between two trees. Whimsy is Willi's addition, with small sculptures sprinkled about. Most striking is a flowerbed—an iron bed buried in the soil, flowers planted in place of a quilt.

THE SECRETS OF SUCCESS

John's mission is to assemble a successful plant collection. "The only real secret to gardening up here is to prepare the soil," he says, "if there is a secret. You simply can't buy a plant and stick it in the ground." Not in the mountains, anyway. There's a reason why wildflowers are profuse in some meadows and lacking in others. Conditions have to be perfect for that Rocky Mountain columbine to take root and bloom. The same holds true for any mountain garden. To have a variety of

Columbines are spectacularly successful at high altitude.

blooms requires simulating the environment hospitable to the plants. To achieve this, John added proper soil and drainage that, together with the cold, would yield the correct conditions for the plants he chose.

Hundreds of plants that thrive here prefer cool summer nights, bloom in a shortened season, and are perennial or biennial rather than annual. Raised beds warm up quickly and drain water readily. Topsoil is laced with mushroom compost. The results are spectacular. Some plants, such as delphiniums, Iceland poppies, and columbines, bloom longer in this garden than in the more moderate climes of the foothills. A quick walk along the town road reveals cottages surrounded by columbines and Iceland or Oriental poppies in vivid rainbow colors. Neighbors watching John's garden have taken note and created stunning gardens of their own.

Many plants are alpine or rock-garden beauties, but not all. Those that are lacking in vigor have been weeded out of John's garden. Daylilies never bloom at high altitude, and foxgloves are damaged by hail. Others you might not expect to thrive have proved to be stalwart. Lilacs bloom at the gateway, the old-fashioned French as well as several Asian varieties. Natives like the Wood's rose—pink wild roses that grow along hiking trails—have been encouraged to stay, as have the native cinquefoil, columbine, and penstemon.

Rock garden plants of succulents, phlox, and Artemisia are planted in gravelly beds for quick drainage.

To augment the soil for his garden, John creates his own homemade compost. A bin in back reveals garden clippings mixed with llama manure from a neighbor's pet. There's not much compost to be generated from John's

A gravel pathway connects garden and forest so that the edges of each blend seamlessly.

garden, but a little goes a long way. With the exception of a small vegetable garden, his plants are hardy and don't cry out for rich soil.

Beds lined with large rocks raise the garden and define the edges. Those in the sun are covered with a mulch of small pebbles, approximately two to four inches thick. Those in the shade receive a mulch of wood chips. Today, the pebble mulch beds contain sun-loving succulents, rock-garden perennials, natives, and all plants that require quick drainage for their roots to thrive. It's also a bed for self-seeding plants because the gravel acts as a nursery for tiny seedlings. These plants grow best in berms, which provide the drainage they need. John has learned that you really can't garden in the mountains unless you build berms for plants. It's somewhat like the side of a mountain. The berms, he claims, warm up faster in the spring, provide decent drainage and some soil. Also, you can dig in a berm to plant bulbs or perennials.

These gravel-covered beds house tulips and ten varieties of daffodils. "Tulips came from the Mesopotamia region originally," John says. "They cannot take too much water on their roots. I plant them anywhere from six to eight to ten inches in depth. They must be deep enough to not bake from the heat or rot from the drainage of an irrigation system. I plant five together in a clump and they will multiply." This could only work with the raised bed system that John uses. Digging ten inches in the rocky soil is impossible.

The wood chip–mulched beds lie under the aspen trees, where they are home to woodland plants. Primroses and ferns form the backbone, joined by coralbells, columbines, and violas. Any natives or perennials that thrive in a cool, shaded area, much like the bank of a river, will take to a woodland bed. In general, they need more water and higher humidity. The wood mulch provides both.

John will trim small trees to keep them tiny. They will never tower over rock garden plants like snow-in-summer.

NOT A STRIP OF GRASS

Surrounding all the beds are gravel walkways. There's not a strip of grass. That saves on water and work. Where the groomed beds end, a small meditative garden of crushed stone edges into the aspen forest.

John points with delight to the native plants that have blown into the garden and taken root. Rather than weed them out, he searches for a way to take them in. Several blue spruce seedlings have sprouted. Instead of allowing a giant tree to grow, he'll trim and transform the small saplings into bonsai, which will create winter architecture in the garden. "The old adage, 'A weed is just a plant out of place,' certainly holds true in my garden," John says, as he notes several native plants that have sprung to life on the gravel paths.

Blue forget-me-nots companion with pink phlox in the woodland gardens.

Rhubarb is planted among the perennials. Although it's an old-fashioned vegetable best enjoyed in pies, it's not

Iceland poppies, like columbine, are more vigorous and bloom longer in John's garden than they might at lower elevations.

suitable for planting in an annual vegetable bed. A small vegetable plot succeeds best with greens: lettuces and spinach. Willi adores sugar snap peas, so there are plenty of those, too.

In the early spring, black plastic is stretched over the bed to warm it. Perhaps growing vegetables is too chancy this high in the mountains, but John has attempted all facets of gardening, and he's convinced that a few green and leafy salads are soul satisfying. "I also add the floating cover over the plants. We have few pests up here; the winters are too cold and long for them to survive. Our greatest pest was a porcupine. But the floating cover does help to preserve the plants from wind and cold."

Often, we overlook how strong the sun can be in Colorado. Plants that require "full sun" in an English garden may do well in shade or part shade here. That simple truth has encouraged John to grow many plants in part shade. Columbines are excellent candidates, but so are delphiniums, tulips, daffodils, and poppies. Even catmint *(Nepeta faassenii)*, well known in xeric sun gardens of lower elevations, grows in part shade.

Most remarkable is the sheer number of plants in the Brocklehurst garden— all on a shoestring budget. Some have been grown from seed and several received as cuttings from friends and neighbors. "I've been a gardener most of my life," John says, "so I've had to economize. I like to point out that it's possible to build a large plant collection with modest means."

A few have been gifts from nature. At the river's edge bloom a group of native shooting stars, their delicate droopy pink and white petals hanging from an arched stem. Seeds blew in and found a comfortable home sheltered from the wind in a challenging but not inhospitable landscape—much like John and Willi themselves.

PLANTS AND FLOWERS

Artemisia (*Artemisia*, many varieties)

Bellflower (*Campanula*, many varieties, from the tiny teacups rock-garden ground cover to larger)

Bishop's weed (*Aegopodium podagraria* 'Variegatum'). A lovely green and white variegated ground cover that is especially hardy.

Bleeding heart (*Dicentra spectabilis*)

Blue flax (*Linum perenne*). Excellent self-seeder.

Bluebells (*Mertensia lanceolata*). A native; seeds blown in.

Candytuft (*Iberis sempervirens*)

Clematis (*Clematis* 'Anna Louise', 'Duchess of Edinburgh')

Coreopsis (*Coreopsis*)

Crocus (*Crocus* bulbs)

Columbine (*Aquilegia*, many varieties)

Catmint (*Nepeta faassenii*)

Coralbells (*Heuchera sanguinea*)

Cinquefoil, leafy (*Drymocallis fissa*)

Daffodil (*Narcissus*, ten varieties)

Delphinium (*Delphinium elatum*, also dwarf)

Dianthus, also called pinks (*Dianthus*, many varieties)

Daisy, painted (*Chrysanthemum coccineum*)

Euphorbia (*Euphorbia*). Eighteen inches high with green and yellow florets; Poisonous.

Fern (*Asplenium* 'Lady's Fern')

Daisy, fleabane (*Erigeron colomexicanus*). A native; seeds blown in.

Forget-me-not (*Myosotis sylvatica*)

Garlic chive (*Allium*, a variety of the smaller varieties)

Gentian (*Gentiana*)

Geranium, hardy (*Geranium* 'Cranesbill' and 'Johnson's Blue')

Grape hyacinth (*Muscari*, many varieties)

Hens and chickens (*Sempervivum*, five varieties)

Hops vine (*Humulus lupulus*)

Lady's mantle (*Alchemilla mollis*)

Lupine (*Lupinus*, Russell hybrids)

Lamb's ears (*Stachys byzantina*)

Leopard's bane (*Doronicum*)

Lilac (*Syringa vulgaris*, and many varieties)

Lily (*Lilium*, Asiatic)

Lily-of-the-valley (*Convallaria majalis*)

Mallow (*Sidalcea malviflora*)

Meadow rue (*Thalictrum aquilegiafolium*)

Obedient plant (*Physotegia virginiana*)

Oregon grape (*Mahonia repens*)

Pansy (*Viola*)

Painted tongue (*Salpiglossis sinuata*). Grown as an annual.

Penstemon (*Penstemon*, many varieties)

Phlox (*Phlox divaricata*)

Peony (*Paeonia herbaceous*)

Pincushion flower (*Scabiosa caucasica*)

Primrose (*Primula polyantha*)

Poppy, Oriental (*Papaver orientale*); Iceland (*Papaver nudicaule*); Himalayan blue (*Meconopsis grandis*)

Rose, wild only (*Rosa woodsii*)

Rudbeckia (*Rudbeckia fulgida* 'Goldstrum')

Strawberry-ornamental. Also known as alpine strawberries or wild strawberries or fraises de bois, these do not bear fruit.

Skullcap (*Scutellaria*)

Showy stonecrop (*Sedum*, many varieties, including 'Autumn Joy')

Shooting star (*Dodecatheon*). A native; seed blown in.

Sweet william (*Dianthus barbatus*)

Snow-in-summer (*Cerastium tomentosum*)

Solomon's seal (*Polygonatum biflorum*)

Soapwort (*Saponaria ocymoides*)

Sulphur-flower (*Eriogonum umbellatum*). A native; seeds blown in.

Tansy *(Tanacetum vulgare)*
Tulip (*Tulipa,* many varieties*)*
Veronica, also called speedwell
(*Veronica,* many varieties)
Viola *(Viola)*
Verbascum, also called mullein
(*Verbascum phoenicium,*
mixed colors)
Windflower *(Anemone)*
Rocket *(Ligularia stenocephala).*
Requires extensive watering.

VEGETABLES AND HERBS

Lettuces, spinach, rhubarb
(a perennial), sugar snap peas,
radishes, arugula, cilantro,
mints (many varieties),
potatoes (Peruvian purple),
thyme (two varieties),
strawberries, carrots, chard

TREES

Mugo pine, aspen, blue spruce,
dwarf Norway spruce, dwarf
Scotch pine

RESOURCES

■ GARDEN CENTERS SPECIALIZING IN HIGH-ALTITUDE PLANTS

Colorado Alpines' Wildflower Farm, 33601 U.S. Highway 6, Edwards, 81632; 970-926-5504.

Natives and alpine plants.

Evergreen Nursery, 26479 Colorado Highway 74, Kittredge, 80457; 303-674-2132;

www.evergreen-nursery.com.

■ HELPFUL ORGANIZATIONS

Alpine Garden Society, AGS Centre, Avon Bank, Pershore, Worcestershire WR10 3JP, United

Kingdom; www.alpinegardensociety.org. An international look at high-altitude gardening.

American Penstemon Society, c/o Ann Bartlett, Secretary, 1569 South Holland Court, Lakewood,

80232. Penstemons are the largest genus of wildflower in the United States; many are suited

for mountain gardening.

Betty Ford Alpine Gardens, 183 Gore Creek Drive, Vail, 81657; 970-476-0103;

www.bettyfordalpinegardens.org. Provides excellent guidance on mountain gardening.

Cooperative Extension, 1 Administration Building, Colorado State University, Fort Collins, 80523;

970-491-6281; www.ext.colostate.edu/pubs/Garden/07406.html. Information on mountain

gardening.

The North American Rock Garden Society, P.O. Box 67, Millwood, New York 10546;

www.nargs.org. A good alpine gardening resource.

ERA OF GENTILITY:
VICTORIANS

■ PRESERVING THE PAST: A VICTORIAN UPDATE

by NIKI HAYDEN

Victorian homes exude self-confidence. Like prima donnas on the opera stage, they fill a street with character. It's easy to succumb to their charms.

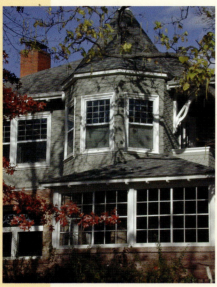

A Victorian with Queen Anne touches blends an eastern architectural style with western building materials.

As familiar as a grandmother, as fragile as an aging screen star, we cherish them and hope they'll live forever.

That's why fans of Victoriana brace themselves for steep prices and lengthy makeovers, as one family did when they took on an 1890 shingle-style home in the foothills of Colorado. "This was a well-loved and beautiful home," says the owner. "We didn't want to disturb those original feelings. The people previous to us had been here for forty years. There was an aura here we didn't want to lose."

The shingle style is associated with windswept ocean coves along Cape Cod, where shingles added a layer of protection against harsh coastal winds. But when this rugged and stark architecture migrated west, it incorporated native materials. In this Victorian, immense red rocks from a local quarry form the foundation. In an East meets West marriage, the soft red tones of sandstone against the pattern of sage green shingles set the stage in a combination not likely to be found outside the Rocky Mountains.

Oversized windows of varying shape and size open the home to light. But the kitchen was a cramped later addition. Bathrooms were skimpy and small. Could this gracious old home with Queen Anne touches be doubled in size and still maintain its original elegance?

Lot Size Determined Changes

Stephen Vosper, one of the principals of Architecture Incorporated in Boulder, walked through the home with his client. From the beginning, he knew the house had two features that would be essential to a large expansion. A huge rectangular lot provided room to grow without disturbing the street front of the home. That would become important to pass reviews by the historical preservation board. And the outside of the house was filled with textures. The surfaces of shingles, rocks, porches, balconies, and bricks could be echoed in the renovations, augmenting the original look of the home.

So Stephen and the homeowners set about to make the house a remodel through sleight-of-hand methods. They added a new kitchen, bathroom, and mudroom in the back of the downstairs. Above the kitchen they added a master bed and bathroom. From the street, you'd never realize the house had been changed at all.

That's a crucial component, because this home was located in a historic district. To make any changes, the architect had to satisfy a city board. Stephen, accustomed to building contemporary homes, knew that he had embarked upon a project different than anything he had tackled before. "It was an education to see the complexity of the issue," he says. "The general idea is to be equitable to everyone, but some situations are easier to work with than others. This was difficult but not out of the ordinary."

Architects capitalized on the many textures of the home: shingles, red rocks, white trim, and siding.

Be Prepared to Spend Time and Money

Buying a Colorado Victorian house is a lot like buying into the historical period: the Victorian era is full of surprises, like borrowed flourishes from previous ages; machine-age fabrication mixed with old world craftsmanship and expertise. You never know quite what to expect until you walk through the premises with an architect.

Outstanding stonework combined with less-than-stellar construction. Remarkable large windows were set above unfinished pine flooring. The original owner sold windows, so he spared no expense for them. They are wide and lavishly appointed all throughout the house. He cared less about centering the parlor fireplace. Electrical wiring and plumbing required updating.

"It took six months for the landmark board and certainly a year after that to do the work. Construction was a long-term process because of the nature of

Homeowners extended the Victorian style in formal outdoor gardens.

these older homes," Stephen says. "The whole thing took about two years. Nine months to eighteen months is what people need to be thinking of. They did strip it down to its bones, rewire, replaster—gave it a new set of clothes good for another hundred years."

The house swelled from 3,400 square feet to about 5,000 with a finished attic and basement, as well as kitchen, bath, mudroom, and upstairs master bed and bathroom. Once the additions were approved, the renovations went smoothly.

A FAMILY HOUSE UPDATED

The most spectacular room is the new kitchen; the most surprising room turned out to be an attic bedroom. The squarish, ample kitchen has built-in cabinets that look to be separate pieces. With glass-paned doors and antique light fixtures, the intention is to give a nod to nineteenth-century style. The attic bedroom transformed a tiny space that now feels like a retreat, brushing the tops of the trees. "There are beautiful little windows that on the outside were only decorative," Stephen says about the eyebrow windows that arch along the roofline.

An outdoor patio blends the home and garden with a continuation of rocks that are sympathetic in color to those originally used as the foundation.

In the end, the homeowners got exactly what they wanted: a family home that will be large enough for extended family and entertaining. One of the hallmarks of this turn-of-the-century home is that once a door is shut, each room is a small world unto itself: parents and friends dining can be shut off from rambunctious teens in the media room. Kitchen gatherings can be informal, while more formal parties take place in the parlor. "That's what makes it such a good family home," Stephen says. "There's a place for everyone."

As for the homeowners, they like the look of a street where each home has a history, comes with a past. In Colorado, a Victorian is just as likely to be nestled next to a bungalow, or across from a colonial. Like the transplants they represent, the 1850s Colorado homes straddle historic styles and pragmatically adapt to the materials of the western landscape.

■ HELPFUL ORGANIZATIONS

Colorado Preservation, Inc., 1900 Wazee Street, Suite 360, Denver, 80202; 303-893-4260;
www.coloradopreservation.org. Offers a wealth of web links and data about current
preservation efforts in Colorado.

Historic Boulder, 646 Pearl Street, Boulder, 80302; 303-444-5192; www.historicboulder.org.
Architectural preservation.

Historic Denver, 1536 Wynkoop Street, Suite 400A, Denver, 80202; 303-534-5288;
http://historicdenver.org. Architectural preservation.

■ IMPORTANT VICTORIAN HOUSES (OPEN TO THE PUBLIC)

Bloom Mansion, 300 East Main Street, Trinidad, 81082; 719-846-7217;
www.coloradohistory.org/hist_sites/trinidad/bloommansion.htm. Part of the Trinidad Museum
complex. An extravagant mansion with remarkable brickwork. Open May through September.

Byers-Evans House Museum, 1310 Bannock Street, Denver, 80204; 303-620-4933. A restored
Victorian mansion with many of its original furnishings.

Molly Brown House, 1340 Pennsylvania Street, Denver, 80203; 303-832-4092;
www.mollybrown.org. The home of Colorado's famous *Titanic* survivor.

Rosemount Museum, 419 West Fourteenth Street, Pueblo, 81003; 719-545-5290;
www.rosemount.org. A stunning Victorian from 1893.

■ VICTORIAN ARTIFACTS AND ACCESSORIES

Architectural Antiques, 2669 Larimer Street, Denver, 80205; 303-297-9722;
www.archantiques.com.

Architectural Artifacts, 2207 Larimer Street, P.O. Box 16541, Denver, 80205; 303-292-6012;
www.abqueencity.com.

Architectural Salvage, 5001 North Colorado Boulevard, Denver, 80216; 303-321-0200.

Architectural Stuff, 3970 South Broadway, Englewood, 80110; 303-761-2999.

Bradbury and Bradbury, P.O. Box 155, Benicia, California 94510; 707-746-1900;

www.bradbury.com. Historic and art wallpaper.

Carter and Company, Mt. Diablo Handprints, 451 Ryder Street, Vallejo, California 94590;

707-554-2682; www.carterandco.com. Historic hand printed wallpaper.

Do-It-Ur-Self Plumbing & Heating Supply, 3120 Brighton Boulevard, Denver, 80216; 303-297-0455.

Antique and reproduction bathroom and kitchen fixtures; reglazing and radiators.

Eron Johnson Antiques, Ltd., 451 Broadway, Denver, 80203; 303-777-8700;

www.eronjohnsonantiques.com.

J.R. Burrows & Company, P.O. Box 522, Rockland, Massachusetts 02370; 800-347-1795;

www.burrows.com. Historic textiles and wallpaper.

McGuckn Hardware, 2525 Arapahoe Avenue, Boulder, 80302; 303-443-1822; www.mcguckin.com.

Wide selection of hard-to-find hardware.

Paris Blue, 350 Kalamath Street, Denver, 80223; 720-932-6200. Specializes in antiques with a

French touch.

Raven Architectural Artifacts, 600 North Second Street, LaSalle, 80645; 970-284-0921.

Rejuvenation House Parts, 2550 Northwest Nicolai Street, Portland, Oregon 97210;

888-401-1900; www.rejuvenation.com. Specializing in vintage lighting reproductions, this

northwestern company began as a house parts salvage operation (which it still operates

alongside its vintage reproductions business). Catalog available free from the website.

Specialty Architectural Products, 2400 East Colfax Avenue, Denver, 80206; 303-316-9300.

The Renovator's Supply, Inc., Renovator's Old Mill, Millers Falls, Massachusetts 01349;

800-659-2211; www.rensup.com. Reproduction of vintage items.

Wise Buys Antiques, 190 Second Avenue, P.O. Box 153, Niwot, 80544; 303-652-2888.

Original fireplace mantels salvaged.

Van Dyke's Restorers, 39771 SD Hwy 34 East, P.O. Box 278, Woonsocket, South Dakota

57385; 800-585-1234; www.vandykes.com. Reproduction of vintage items.

■ DEEP ROOTS:
REDISCOVERING GRANDMOTHER'S GARDEN

by NIKI HAYDEN

Your grandmother's Victorian garden originated from hardy stock. Not all the toughest plants around are natives—plants that originated here. Some of the old heirlooms—plants that are at least one hundred years old and may have been imported from anywhere else in the world—have adapted to Front Range soil, aridity, and cold. They made an entrance in the nineteenth century, and they're still around today. You'll see them planted at the foundation of old farmhouses—tall bearded irises or a thorny rose cascading over the porch. Today, collectors of historic irises are nostalgic for their grandmother's garden and, to ensure hardy survivors, are dedicated to preserving those with the toughest genes.

Bearded irises are among the toughest plants that can be grown along the Front Range.

If your house is Victorian, consider some of your grandmother's favorites—irises, lilacs, and hardy roses. They're long-lived, easy to grow, and splashy. Most won't bloom for the entire summer, but they will provide a spectacular bloom that marks a season. You'll know exactly what month it is. Many are grown locally, so you'll receive a sturdy rootstock.

Bearded irises are among the hardiest perennials to grow along Colorado's Front Range, but at Long's Iris Gardens in Boulder, crows have ripped the young shoots from their neat rows.

"My husband and I have taken to having our dinner out here and waiting for nightfall," says owner Catherine Long Gates, where she stands watch until the vandalizing crows retire to their nests.

This is a new problem for Catherine, one she has never encountered on this third-generation iris farm. Crows are about the only pests that will attack the plants, and that's because these wholesale-

Hardy roses can be as tough as bearded irises.

grown irises stand at attention like toy soldiers. Crows, smart-aleck birds that they are, have decided to play with the tender shoots. As soon as the irises grow a bit larger, they'll be left alone.

Even deer won't eat irises or narcissi. "That's because there's something toxic in the two plants that deer don't like," Catherine says, and this is just one reason why she can raise bearded irises for wholesale along the Front Range.

The truth is, bearded irises are nearly perfectly adapted to the soil, arid weather, and critter conditions in this part of the world. They're drought-tolerant plants, often grown in the median of a highway. You'll find historic irises on abandoned Colorado farms. And irises most often are recommended for that difficult patch of ground: dry, gravelly strips that run between sidewalks and streets.

Botanists say that although the large iris family includes varieties that adore swampy land or humid climates, the bearded iris originated somewhere between the Mediterranean and Turkey. Bearded irises were born in a climate much like our own, naturally hybridized from as many as fourteen wild irises. According to folklore, when Louis VII discovered irises in Egypt during the Crusades, he brought them back to France. Iris became the *fleur-de-lis*, or flower-of-Louis, that graced his coat of arms.

MOST UNDERAPPRECIATED PERENNIAL

Bearded irises are so successful in Colorado that they're often unappreciated. That's a shame, because there's a wide selection of tall, intermediate, and dwarf varieties.

The distinctive beard comes from the furry tongues on the sepals that brush pollen onto the legs of helpful insects. The only difference among the bearded irises is that dwarf cultivars require less division.

While newly hybridized irises don't have the staying power of the old-fashioned "flags," as they were once termed, most bearded irises will bloom, thrive, and multiply with little effort on the gardener's part.

Still, the large, showy bearded irises that Long's Iris Gardens features are less in demand these days. "Everyone is going to smaller yards," Catherine says. "Now we're growing more dwarf and intermediate iris. And I'm looking into Siberian and beardless iris that don't need much dividing. They do have a higher water requirement, and that is a big deal for us.

"It's the old historic iris that you'll see blooming on Colorado homesteads," Catherine continues. "The modern hybridized iris might grow just fine, but

Iris was the Greek goddess of the rainbow, an apt name for the spectrum of colors available.

probably wouldn't bloom. That's because they must be divided about every four years. They do need some water, especially in the spring, and I advise people to mix their soil with a little compost.

"We divide and plant in the spring, although iris can be planted in the fall. The second year after planting, you can add some phosphorus fertilizer. They'll also benefit from a little nitrogen, but not too much. Otherwise, the growth is too soft and the leaves grow at the expense of the bloom. Also, too much nitrogen makes it susceptible to rot, as does too much water."

Old-fashioned blue irises, with tall swords, add architectural interest to a garden.

Bearded irises languish in hot, humid, or rainy climates. Southern gardeners fuss over them, complaining about diseases and rot. But along the Front Range, that won't happen, providing you don't plant your irises next to a heavily watered lawn, or in a low spot that collects water.

The soil of the foothills and plains is nearly ideal: high in potassium, weak in nitrogen. Catherine says that simply moving irises every so often appears to rejuvenate the plant. To prevent water evaporation, cut the leafy fans back by a third when dividing. The bulbous base of corms soaks up energy from the sun, storing nutrients for the plant. It's essential that the corms rest on the surface of the soil and not be covered by dirt or mulch. Good drainage and full sun are required. Rocky soil is adored.

Catherine has taken to spreading alfalfa pellets as a fertilizer. This has become a trend among growers, she says, because the pellets may contain minerals in trace amounts that irises need. She also sows winter rye, buckwheat, peas, or vetch as cover crops to add a bit of nitrogen and to halt soil erosion. Although irises will not thrive in nitrogen-rich soil (they grow loose, floppy leaves and are subject to insect infestations in such conditions), they do need a small amount of the element, as do nearly all plants.

Some Amateur Gardeners Protecting Historic Irises

Like some modern roses, the fragrance of iris has been hybridized out. Traditionally, irises never were known for their fragrance in the same way as the rose, but there are historic *Iris pallida* that exude a grapey scent.

Most iris gardeners are enthusiastic amateurs who aim for extravagant colors and frilled or ruffled petals rather than scent. But because there is renewed interest in historic iris, *pallida* is returning to popularity.

Lilacs: Praise for a Modest Shrub

Lilacs show off their finery once a year. Bold, pendulous blooms studded with tiny flowers perfume the air. The scent is heady, luxurious, and familiar. For a few weeks each spring we're forced to praise this modest shrub.

European lilacs originated in the cold, mountainous Balkans. They're called French lilacs only because the French hybridized and popularized them in their scented gardens. Our climate closely matches the topography and conditions of their home, so you'll find that pests or diseases that attack lilacs—such as powdery mildew—are less likely here than in the South or East. And since lilacs require a cold spell to set blooms, you won't find them in hot desert regions.

Lilacs like full sun and good drainage, and, once established, most common lilacs are drought tolerant. Old reliable lilacs send up suckers to ensure their survival. They'll live for a hundred years or more, rarely depend upon fertilizers, and prefer slightly alkaline soil.

Lilacs Also Come in Yellow and White

"I have planted lilacs without soil amending and they do just fine," says Kerrie B. Badertscher, a horticultural extension agent for Colorado State University. She grows an array of lilacs in her own yard, mostly from cuttings. But buying shrubs in one- to three-gallon containers will work well, too. "I recommend growing them small and letting them get established here," she says.

Growing lilacs from cuttings allows them to thrive on their own roots, which makes them hardier in fierce winters. It's worthwhile to avoid grafted lilacs. If you do intend to amend your soil, Kerrie suggests adding no more than one-third compost mixed well into the native soil. You want the shrub to extend roots farther than just the amended area.

Most gardeners are familiar with the old-fashioned common lilac, *Syringa vulgaris,* and its traditional lavender blooms. This dependable shrub also comes in pink, violet blue, purplish blue, magenta, yellow, and white. All are hardy.

Lilacs can be divided between the European stock, sometimes called French or common lilacs, and those from Asia. Both immigrants are equally tough in our part of the world. Planting several kinds will extend the blooming period because the Asian lilacs usually bloom later than the common. They also are more mildly scented than the common lilac, and in slightly different shades of colors. Only two lilac species come from Europe, but twenty-one are from Asia, so there's an array of Asian lilacs yet to be tried in the New World.

The common French lilac is a sturdy shrub joined by newer immigrants just as carefree—the Asian lilacs.

"The *Syringa patula,* or 'Miss Kim', is a slow-growing small shrub and will stay just three to five feet. Compare that to the common lilac that will get as high as twelve to fifteen feet," Kerrie says. "I just love this plant and have several. I've not seen powdery mildew, nor insects, neither winter dieback nor chlorosis. It's just a wonderful rounded shape and requires very little care. It also provides a reddish fall foliage. I think it could be tricky to transplant. But for a small shrub I recommend it."

She also grows the Asian tree lilacs, or *Syringa reticulata* (Japanese lilac) and *Syringa pekinensis* (Pekin lilac). The Pekin lilac grows to a height of fifteen to twenty feet. The Japanese lilac may reach twenty to thirty feet. "This one is a little different," she says about the Pekin lilac. "It has a bark with a cherry color. And that's one of the ornamental features. It blooms in early summer, with a light fragrance. The bark exfoliates and it's shiny and brown, lending itself to a striking winter texture."

The Japanese lilac also has a cherry-colored bark. Both grow best in full sun, are winter hardy, mostly pest free, and well adapted to alkaline soil. They do require more water than the common lilac.

Lilacs Are Hardy but Need Checking

"Occasionally we have lilac ash borers," Kerrie says. "You would prune out the affected canes. My feeling is that pruning out a third of the oldest growth will maintain its shape and size—and lessen any need for pesticides. You're pruning out the stressed wood and opening it up for light and air."

Powdery mildew most often attacks a lilac growing in the shade. It rarely does permanent harm, but to deter it, avoid using nitrogen fertilizers and watering excessively around the plant.

If your lilac hasn't bloomed, it's usually the casualty of growing in a shaded area, ill-advised pruning, or a late frost. Kerrie prunes her shrubs by cutting flowers in the spring. If you wait until the blossoms are spent to prune your lilac, you may be cutting off the blooms that have been set for the next year. When you do prune, don't prune the suckers unless you're trying to shape the bush—they help to rejuvenate the shrub. That's the reason lilacs can live so long.

Sometimes a late frost will nip the buds of lilacs, and blossoms won't occur in the spring. Asian varieties often escape this fate because they are late bloomers.

Also, if there's been little snow throughout the winter, you might try watering the shrubs every couple of weeks. Most established common lilacs don't require much watering at all, but make an exception for the Asian varieties.

BADERTSCHER'S RECOMMENDED LILACS FOR COLORADO'S FRONT RANGE

COMMON OR FRENCH LILACS

Syringa vulgaris: French or common lilac

White: 'Ellen Willmott', a double; 'Mont Blanc', a single

Violet: 'Violetta', a double; 'Cavour', a single

Blue: 'Olivier De Serres', a double; 'President Lincoln', a single

Pink: 'Fantasy', a double; 'Lucie Baltet', a single

Magenta: 'Charles Joly', a double; 'Congo', a single

Yellow: 'Primrose', a single

ASIAN LILACS

Syringa patula: Manchurian or Korean lilac

Blue purple: 'Miss Kim'

Syringa reticulata: Japanese lilac

Yellow to creamy: 'Chantilly Lace', 'China Gold'

Syringa pekinensis: Pekin lilac, only a few cultivars are available;
   often, it will take several years before this lilac begins to bloom.

HARDY ROSES HAVE A PLACE IN THE COLORADO LANDSCAPE

Roses unfairly carry a reputation as fussy and finicky—especially in Colorado. Consider that more than two thousand cultivars of roses grow in the world today, and many have yet to be attempted in a Colorado climate. This is unfortunate, because roses have been cultivated historically in climates much like our own. For example, in dry and chilly northern Iran, the image of the rose adorns painted teahouses and plays a prominent role in walled gardens.

Roses may be the most beloved and one of the sturdiest flowers throughout history. The blossoms of old-fashioned species roses, such as the bright-red Austrian copper or Harison's yellow, spill over many a rickety turn-of-the-century farm fence.

Hardy shrub roses offer disease resistance, are often repeat bloomers, and require less water and fertilizer than hybrid tea roses.

With a shrub that has lasted so long and covers such a vast geographical stretch, there's a rose for everyone, even on the Front Range.

Newcomers to Colorado are tempted to cultivate roses only to discover that the plants die during their first winter. Perhaps the temperature dropped fifty degrees in one day, killing one of the more tender bushes. Or the rose wasn't hardened off in mid-August before early autumn cold. Maybe watering was overlooked during a dry spell.

Even skilled gardeners may lose some of their hybrid tea or grandiflora roses during a harsh winter. It's not always the cold that's the culprit, it's also severe winds and dry winters.

Don't Despair

Growing roses in Colorado requires a different way of thinking. The most commonly found rose, the hybrid tea, wasn't introduced until 1867. Most hardy roses either predate the hybrid tea or belong to the modern revamped shrub roses with a gene pool dating back to the hardiest of the rose stock.

Instead of the popular hybrid tea roses, consider the modern shrub choices of Canadian, Griffith Buck, and David Austin roses. Canadian roses—bred for hardiness, disease resistance, and repeat bloom—are favorites. The quality they lack is fragrance.

Fragrance often is the first characteristic to be lost in hybridizing flowers. Among the rose genes, fragrance is a recessive trait, so it gives way to hardiness or disease resistance. If fragrance is important, take a look at the old garden roses. Many are raised for their heady perfume, but they often bloom only once, generally in the spring.

Consider what Colorado does offer: fewer rose diseases associated with humid climates. And while some roses need considerable fertilizer and water, others, like the hardiest shrub roses, require less water and little fertilizer. What all roses do share is a need for excellent drainage and at least six to eight hours of bright sunlight daily.

Tips for Planting Roses

Much of Colorado soil is heavy clay. Although clay holds water well, it may also prevent air from circulating around the roots. Roses need oxygen as much as water, so good drainage is essential. The solution to both clay and sandy soil is to add organic matter.

Spring is the most common time to plant roses, particularly bare root. Container roses should be planted after the frost date, usually May 15. Dig a hole about eighteen inches across and twelve inches deep. Mix your original soil so that at least a third is compost. Some rosarians add pebbles to enhance drainage and improve air circulation.

Water deeply, but seldom. Test the soil for dryness by sticking a finger in the top three inches. Constant watering deprives the plants of oxygen and contributes to fungal diseases.

"Own root" roses are gaining in popularity, which indicates that a fancy rose has not been grafted onto a hardy ho-hum rootstock. If the grafted half of the rose is too delicate for a cold Colorado winter, the top of the rose dies. The grafted root will send up a shoot that looks nothing like the rose you originally purchased.

Each year, garden centers carry a wider selection of roses, and buyers learn, through trial and error, what grows best in their gardens. Hardy roses, with their undemanding habits, usually need less pesticide and fungicide to thrive.

A ROSTER OF ROSES

Roses originated with the wild species, or single-petal roses similar to the rugosas that can be found today. When gardeners noticed a few doubled blooms, these tough plants became the basis for hybridization. Although there are more than fifty categories of rose, here are the most common:

Hybrid tea is the traditional garden show rose, and some are notoriously difficult to winter over in Colorado. Often, they comprise a pretty rose grafted to a hardy stock. Rose lovers mound up dirt around the base, mulch generously, and water regularly throughout the winter. When all else fails, they grow them as annuals. Hybrid tea and grandiflora climbers are at particular risk because they set their blooms on old stalks that may be desiccated by dry winds. There are some sturdy hybrid tea cultivars. Rose expert Joan Franson recommends 'Mister Lincoln', 'Yankee Doodle', and 'Pristine'.

Floribundas are a cross between the polyantha and hybrid tea. Frequently a good choice in mass planting.

Grandifloras are a cross between hybrid teas and floribundas. With characteristics similar to the hybrid tea, some are difficult to grow successfully in Colorado.

Polyanthas are hardier than hybrid tea, although only a small number thrive in Colorado. These bushes are used as landscape roses.

Modern shrubs are a diverse group from mixed parentage meant to improve upon the old-fashioned shrub. These roses often bloom throughout an entire season, and many are extremely hardy on the Front Range. Recommended are the Canadian hardy roses ('Winnipeg Parks', 'John David', 'Henry Kelsey'—Canadian roses are named after explorers or parks); also the roses of 'Griffith Buck', 'Applejack', and David Austin 'Abraham Darby'.

Miniature roses are typically tough plants, despite their size. They mimic other roses, and the micros will show best in an alpine garden. Often, they won't remain miniatures. The flowers will stay small, but the bush will grow large. Joan Franson especially recommends 'Jeanne Lajoie', a miniature climber (see interview on page 48).

With so many roses to choose from, there's one that will fit most gardens.

Climbing and rambling roses may include roses from other categories that grow long canes. Ramblers' canes aren't as long as climbers', but roses don't actually "climb." Their canes must be tied to a trellis to achieve the desired effect. They may include bush hybrid teas, grandifloras, or floribundas—none of which are recommended for Colorado gardens.

Old garden roses is a catch-all term for roses hybridized prior to 1867 and some of the earliest cultivars from the species roses. The gallica, alba, Portland, centifolia, Bourbon, moss, damask, and hybrid perpetual are among those generally hardy in Colorado and sometimes called heirloom roses.

Species are the original roses, usually with rose hips, which help create an excellent bird habitat. They're extremely hardy.

An Interview with Rose Expert Joan Franson

Joan Franson teaches classes in rose culture at the Denver Botanic Gardens. Past president of the Colorado Federation of Garden Clubs and a judge for the American Rose Society, she grows a variety of roses in her Arvada garden.

Front Range Living (FRL): What are your favorite roses for your own garden in Arvada?

Joan Franson (JF): I like everything, probably because I'm a rose judge and instructor. My favorite is not the hybrid tea, although they're lovely. But I grow two hundred bushes that include old garden roses, also shrub and floribunda roses.

I especially enjoy the history and the taxonomy of the rose family. I like the stories behind the old garden roses; then people get a wider appreciation of roses. Of our hardiest roses, we have species roses, and there are four species native to Colorado. Those take anything.

Colorado is important in rose history. They have found rose fossil leaves forty million years old, as dated by the Smithsonian. Some of the roses we grow now came from Afghanistan, like the 'Austrian Copper'. And 'Harison's Yellow' the pioneers brought. We have roses that Josephine [of Napoleon Bonaparte fame] had in her garden.

Roses have gone in and out of favor. In the churchyards, monks would grow them for the medicinal value of their hips. Roses are native to the Northern Hemisphere only, but they grow wherever they are introduced.

And there are Canadian hardies, two major groups, which, once established, will practically grow in concrete. They will take bitter cold and are so abundant they can get up to ten feet high and wide.

FRL: You have said that overall design is as important as the roses you choose. What should gardeners keep in mind?

JF: With roses there are so many textures of leaves and varying forms, like upright and arching. I always try to remind people that hybrid teas grow in things other than beds. The hybrid tea grandiflora tend to be more awkwardly upright, compared to the David Austin roses. (David Austin has hybridized roses in England and many grow well in Colorado. Sometimes they are referred to as English roses and fall into the category of a modern shrub rose.)

But with the English or Austin, you can't assume that that's how they all are. David Austin used such a mixed bag over thirty-five years of hybridizing them.

Now some of the big companies are offering their romantic series, which are similar to the Austin roses. They are doing their own hybridizing. David Austin did pioneering work and has dozens and dozens of roses out. The big companies are following his example because not everyone is charmed by a hybrid tea. They are learning to appreciate more than one flower form.

Keep in mind that not every shrub rose is hardy here. 'Graham Thomas' is a luscious butterscotch gold, but it will take a little extra protection for the winter, and you'll have to pay a little more attention to its growth habits. It will grow tall and skinny, with one blossom at the top. After all, Austin hybridized in England. Some things translate and some things don't.

FRL: Miniatures are hardier than people might think, but do all of them grow large?
JF: You can get some that stay under six inches, but others grow large. One you must try is 'Jeanne Lajoie'. It's a pink hybrid tea miniature climber; that is, it mimics the hybrid tea form. It's marvelous. The overall size of the bush can be six to ten feet. Usually miniatures are hardy, but not all.

FRL: When do you fertilize and what kind of fertilizer do you use?
JF: Spring is a good time to fertilize roses, or after they bloom, to bring them through next year. If it blooms only once, I only fertilize once. I prefer organic fertilizers, but I have nothing against chemicals. The difference is that with organics, you are also improving the soil. Chemical fertilizers are just for the bloom.

I use the Mile High Rose Feed fertilizer from the Front Range Rose Society, based on Colorado-grown alfalfa with high protein and the least amount of weed seed. We've recently added sea kelp and a very specific bone meal. If you contact anyone in the Rose Society, they will sell it or tell you where to buy it. I think it's great. We've fine-tuned it for this climate. I use it on perennials and young trees. It's just a good organic fertilizer for roses. You can get it at several garden centers.

FRL: Do you amend your soil when you plant roses?

JF: About twenty-five to thirty percent of your soil can be amended (with compost). I always like to keep two-thirds of the original soil; you don't want to create a clay pot. We are lucky here in Colorado because we have much less disease. Mine have to survive on tough love. Last year I didn't spray anything.

Plant them well and water them well. Check through the winter. Dig down and feel if it's moist.

FRL: Do you have favorites that you recommend?

Many modern shrub roses provide hardiness with extended bloom.

JF: 'Jeanne LaJoie' and 'Sally Holmes' for arching climbers. The rugosa roses are single and double white, pink, and maroon colors. One hybrid tea that would be tough is 'Yankee Doodle'. You don't feed that one. It's disease resistant, not a fancy hybrid tea. 'Mister Lincoln' is a good old standby. 'Pristine' is white with the outer row pink. I like to group for landscape purposes. We have two beds in front because we don't have a backyard. We do it that way for easier care. The shrubs I put in miscellaneous groups.

FRL: What are the most important things to remember with roses?

JF: Water deeply and seldom. Grow them a little lean. Feel the ground; the first inch can be dry, but under that it should be moist. They do like water but they don't want to sit in it. Drainage is so important.

Put rocks in the hole as you plant them because we are on pure clay in Arvada.

If you have any doubt about a place, roses need six hours of sun. There are a few kinds that will grow in light shade, but they bloom more in sun. And good air circulation is important. Poor air circulation will lead to spider mites. Buy several pots and grow them and find out where they are happy. Are they reaching way out and not blooming much? Then you know to move them.

Watch out for competing roots, like right next to a privet hedge. Don't water them like the grass.

FRL: Many of the modern shrubs no longer carry fragrance—that's been hybridized out of them. Is there any chance that will change?

JF: Canadian roses are coming back with fragrance. It's a gambler's choice, but once they've established hardiness, they can work on fragrance. Among the hybrid teas, there's 'Mister Lincoln', 'Oklahoma', and 'Sutter's Gold'. On the shrub list is 'Desiree Parmentier', which blooms only once. On the horizon, look for old-fashioned roses to improve, with greater disease resistance and more fragrance.

FRL: Is there a public rose garden on the Front Range that inspires you?

JF: The Jefferson County Jail started a rose garden in 1993. It's the best garden in Colorado. They have twenty-five hundred rosebushes. Inmates go through a training program. It has changed the whole jail's attitude toward the public. Now they want people to come and see. It's a great morale booster, with six rolling acres in front of the jail.

The Jefferson County Detention Center is in Golden. Take West U.S. Highway 6 past U.S. Highway 40. Continue west to Jefferson County Parkway. Turn north and follow Jefferson County Parkway one-half mile to the Jefferson County Sheriff's Office. Roses begin blooming in early spring and continue through the early fall. Open to the public.

RESOURCES

■ HELPFUL ORGANIZATIONS

Cooperative Extension, 1 Administration Building, Colorado State University, Fort Collins, 80523; 970-491-6281; www.coopext.colostate.edu.

Denver Botanic Gardens, 1005 York Street, Denver, 80206; 720-865-3500; www.denverbotanicgardens.org. Hosts a site for the Denver Rose Society, which recommends rose feed that is best for our growing conditions. Pick up *Growing Roses in Colorado* compiled by the Denver Rose Society, a small booklet that can be purchased through the Society. Contact them through the Denver Botanic Gardens.

The International Lilac Society, c/o Robert Hoepfl, 24 Vince Drive, Rochester, NY 14606; www.lilacs.freeservers.com.

■ SOURCES FOR PLANTS

Harlequin's Gardens, 4795 North 26th Street, Boulder, 80301; 303-939-9403; www.harlequinsgardens.com. Hardy roses, xeric plants, and natives.

Long's Iris Gardens, 3240 Broadway, Boulder, 80303; 303-442-2353; www.longsgardens.com. These wholesale gardens are open to the public from 9 A.M. to 5 P.M., seven days a week, May and June.

■ MAIL-ORDER NURSERY

High Country Roses, Split Mountain Garden Center, 9211 East U.S. Highway 40, Jensen, Utah 84035; 800-552-2082; www.highcountryroses.com. A source for hardy roses acclimated to high altitude.

■ WEBSITE

GardenWeb; www.gardenweb.com. Covers nearly everything about gardening; includes forums.

■ HOVERHOME: A TRIBUTE TO THE TUDOR

by NIKI HAYDEN

Colorado trades on its frontier days: hard-drinking miners, saloon brawls, and mountain men. Less familiar is the backlash against this rugged life, which flooded the state with respectability between the years of 1880 and 1920. Tea at the Brown Palace in Denver? Perhaps an elegant suite at the Jerome in Aspen, or Shakespearean readings at the Chautauqua in Boulder?

No culture appealed quite so keenly to Colorado settlers as the gentility of the British. Import the civilized culture of afternoon tea, perennial flowerbeds, Shakespeare's sonnets, English architectural styles— and surely the West would be tamed.

Many British-influenced homes have made way for office buildings and housing developments. The

The stately Hoverhome combines a Victorian Tudor exterior with a craftsman interior.

grandest of the hotels adapted and flourished. But you'll have to search to find the old Tudor and neo-Gothic styles so beloved by the British and imported to Colorado by easterners. The neo-Tudor style came into vogue around the same time that the craftsman style swept America. Both were English influences at the turn of the twentieth century.

The Victorians loved to imitate previous architectural styles, often choosing a few details borrowed from the past that would recollect that previous age. Tudor-style architecture usually required an imposing entrance with high-pitched roofs. Some included half-timbering, the exposed lumber that forms patterns in buildings from Elizabethan days. The Tudor–inspired Hoverhome in Longmont, while it does not have the distinctive half-timbering feature, does have the pointed, high-pitched roof, the imposing entrance, moldings around the doors and porches, and flat arches that imitate Tudor castles. This marvelous house has survived through the serendipity of the St. Vrain Historical Society, and it is now open to the public.

Hoverhome might be less important as a single structure. Because it's an intact farmstead that has retained original buildings, Hoverhome ranks as an important historical site.

A FAMILY HOME AND FARMSTEAD

In 1914, Charles and Katherine Hover built Hoverhome for $22,000. The site was a 160-acre plot, and back then Hover Road was narrow and unpaved. Although Charles was wealthy from a wholesale pharmaceutical business in Denver, he hoped to manage a modern farm, seizing the scientific thinking of his time— rotating crops, raising sheep for fertilizer as well as wool, growing alfalfa as a nitrogen-fixing crop. Both Charles and Katherine prided themselves on contributing to progress in a rural community and pressed the town for running water and sewage hookup, despite their remote location.

The story takes an interesting twist when Charles and Katherine met nine-year-old Beatrice. With no children of their own, the couple instantly loved the orphaned girl. "She came for a visit and never left," says St. Vrain Historical Society board member Margaret Lindblom, who collected newspaper accounts about Beatrice before her death several years ago.

Beatrice adored her parents as much as they loved her. She never married, remaining with her parents and caring for them as they aged. Beatrice and

Katherine gardened, shared favorite books, dedicated themselves to civic projects, and grew old together in their elegant farmhouse. Most of the farmland was sold to a church-sponsored nursing home, where Beatrice lived the last ten years of her life. "Beatrice died in 1991," Margaret says. "She was in her nineties and never mentioned her life before the Hovers."

Yellow roses, possibly Harison's rose, can be found in the stained glass windows and china pattern. Yellow roses were planted on the fencing in front.

TRAPPED IN TIME

The house, barn, nearby cottage, and gardens eventually were purchased by the historical society, which now maintains the property for the public. The site is listed on the National Register of Historic Places not simply because of the grand home, but because the barn, gardens, and property surround a farmstead that remains intact and remarkably close to the original.

A tour through Hoverhome reveals that little has changed. Beatrice maintained her adopted family home as if it were a museum, trapped in a period of time—her childhood—when Tiffany lamps arrived via rail, Limoges china painted with yellow roses set the table, and stained glass windows of yellow roses cast a soft glow on the oak balustrade.

The theme of yellow roses repeats with Harison's yellow roses lining the

Tea is set, as it might have been nearly a century ago.

fence along Hover Road, now a major street in Longmont. In back, the outlines of a formal rose garden surround a birdbath. A seventeenth-century English sundial measures time against a backdrop of French lilacs and tall bearded irises. Red peonies edge a walkway, and rows of catalpa trees serve as a canopy, strewing long bean pods onto the lawn.

Inside the house, you'll find the original bathroom tiles and bathtubs—no showers. The kitchen boasts all the amenities of the time: built-in flour

Little has been altered in the house, as if Beatrice wanted to preserve her upbringing.

bins, a small door to haul ice for an icebox, and a coal stove. Narrow stairs lead to a servant's apartment above. "The maid's quarters was going out of vogue at the time; that has overtones of the Victorian," says architectural engineer Richard Beardmore, whose Fort Collins firm is dedicated to historical preservation. "This is a unique place. You don't see many homes of this stature and size in that period in a rural setting. To find a farmstead professionally designed is unusual."

Hoverhome reflects the arts and crafts period, so popular in England in the late nineteenth and early twentieth century and easily adapted to American tastes. Arts and crafts originated in England, the product of designer William Morris's creative genius. As a reaction against the fussiness and industrialization of the Victorians, Morris stressed handcrafted furnishings. He relied upon artistic elements from the Gothic and medieval periods when the hand of the maker reigned. Later luminaries like Frank Lloyd Wright would benefit from the arts and crafts aesthetic and shepherd its guiding principles in American art and architecture.

"It's still very livable. The Hovers retained an architect with more modern views than his time,' explains Beardmore. "This style goes in and out of vogue, but many of the people who like the bungalow style find warmth in the wood and textures of the house. The house reflects a pastoral setting for Katherine's interest in the arts and Charles's scientific interests."

Katherine's writing desk, with family photos, looks as if she has just stepped away.

American bungalow fans cite large hearths, built-in oak bookcases, and stained glass windows as examples of cozy, handcrafted appeal. Hoverhome is no exception. For a six-thousand-square-

A handsome wire hearth grating, like the craftsman style of the period, shows attention to handcrafted details.

foot house, it remains warm and inviting with a magnificent hearth, stenciled bedroom walls, lustrous oak balustrade, and richly patterned Oriental carpets.

Our tour guide, Margaret, points to all the exterior doors. Rooms were "meant to flow from inside to the outside," she says. Tuberculosis was the scourge of the age; fresh air the perceived prevention. Most downstairs rooms have doors leading out, and second-story rooms offer balconies. Transom windows above the interior doors allow fresh air to circulate through the house.

MUSIC AND BOOKS

When Beatrice reached her eighties, she began to sell and give away furniture, then in a change of heart, left some pieces in the house. The Hovers' bedroom glows with a sunny gold yellow paint, Katherine's delicate floral stenciling strung high along the walls. The portraits of a young Katherine and Charles glance into the room. Their marriage certificate hangs framed on the wall.

It's Katherine's personality more than Beatrice's or Charles's that dominates the house today. Her petite dress form stands in a room arranged for a seamstress. She also loved music, and her piano sits in the living room—a Steinway Duo-Art reproducing piano. Several Victrolas were found throughout the house as evidence that music filled Hoverhome. A record is poised to play "Silent Night."

Katherine painted her Victorian bedroom in a sunny yellow and stenciled a stylized flower design along the walls.

If music was Katherine's muse, books enthralled Beatrice. Her bedroom includes a library. Reading influenced her life, and she fashioned a career transcribing books into Braille for the blind. Both Katherine and Beatrice gardened in the conservatory—a must for any British–inspired home. Today it shelters red geraniums and blue hydrangeas. Alongside the driveway, a rustic shed houses antique garden tools.

By itself, Hoverhome might only reveal a home of the rich and fashionable. True, it's an authentic example of the American arts and crafts period. But with a modest house next door and a barn, mill, creamery, and

Katherine's presence remains throughout the house.

chicken house, the farmstead includes a glimpse of several families. The 1902 cottage became the home of their tenant farmworkers. The household workers, farmworkers, and Hovers lived closely, yet separately, in divided lives.

And while not on the grand scale of the British gentry, Hoverhome replicates social divisions that also marked American society during that time. Beatrice preserved for posterity her enchanted world. This was a home that invited an orphan into the hearts and house of a privileged couple—a home so remarkable that she decided never to leave.

RESOURCES

Hoverhome, 1309 Hover Road, Longmont, 80501; 303-774-7810; www.stvrainhistoricalsociety.org/ Hoverhome.htm. Hoverhome is available for weddings and hosts occasional teas.

■ HELPFUL ORGANIZATIONS

St. Vrain Historical Society, P.O. Box 705, Longmont, 80501; 303-776-1870; www.stvrainhistoricalsociety.org.

Every downstairs room has a door leading outside. Fresh air was the antidote to tuberculosis at that time.

■ BLOOMS AND THE BARD: A SHAKESPEARE GARDEN

by DIANE ZUCKERMAN

Casually dressed in a T-shirt and shorts, a baseball cap shielding his eyes from the late afternoon sun, the middle-aged man strolled into the courtyard. Walking past the flowerbed that held a large stone engraved with the words "Shakespeare Gardens," he stopped to watch as several gardeners settled a bushy rosemary shrub into its new surroundings.

Shakespeare Gardens is associated with the Colorado Shakespeare Festival at the University of Colorado in Boulder.

Glancing about with a puzzled look, the man quietly asked, as though thinking aloud, "What makes this a Shakespearean garden?"

Right on cue, Marlene Cowdery turned from supervising the planting, face brightening like a teacher whose new pupil has just asked the best of all possible questions.

"We plant plants that were familiar to Shakespeare," Marlene answered simply. With a welcoming smile, she walked over to the man, warming to the opportunity to share her horticultural passion with another visitor to the colorful gardens tucked behind the Hellems building on the University of Colorado's Boulder campus.

The Colorado Shakespeare Gardens are associated with the Colorado Shakespeare Festival. The gardens sprouted from a tiny seed planted in 1990, when Marlene suggested the idea to festival artistic director, Richard Devin.

Shakespeare Festival also Celebrates the Bard as Gardener

For Marlene, a longtime Boulder resident, the gardens are a way to express her combined love of herbs, gardening, and Shakespeare's works. For visitors, the gardens enrich the experience of seeing the festival's four annual productions, presented in repertory at the Mary Rippon Outdoor Theatre and University Theatre on the Boulder campus.

The gardens were officially established in 1991, and the first plantings took root in the spring of 1992. Membership in the nonprofit Colorado Shakespeare Gardens is now about thirty people. Membership dues and private donations fund the projects, with many plantings rotated to represent each season's plays. The public is welcome to visit the garden at any time.

It's surprising to learn how many different plants—at least 180—Shakespeare actually mentioned in his work. "So much of his writing is from an aspect of a gardener," Marlene says. "If he mentions a plant, it's for a very, very good reason, because it involves the plant and part of the play." One of the Bard's best-known floral-inspired lines appears in *Hamlet* when Ophelia, following her father's death, observes, "There's rosemary, that's for remembrance; pray you, love, remember."

Another example is Shakespeare's reference to the herb sampire (also spelled samphire), which has been planted in the gardens to mark *King Lear*.

All the roses in Shakespeare Gardens are either mentioned in the original plays, or are recent roses named after a Shakespearean character, such as 'Juliet', a modern shrub rose.

A few modern English roses evoke the names of famous characters in William Shakespeare's plays.

Sometimes called sea fennel, sampire is a slender succulent with gray green leaves that usually is found along the seashore. In *King Lear*, it plays a part in revealing the recently blinded Gloucester's precarious emotional state. Trying to cope with Gloucester's insistence on jumping to his death, his son Edgar pretends they are standing at the edge of a steep cliff, where "Half way down hangs one that gathers sampire, dreadful trade!"

Roses Illustrate English History

The Bard's *Richard II* follows the shift in power between warring royal factions. The House of Lancaster is represented by a red rose, *Rosa gallica* var. *officinalis*, the House of York by a white one, *Rosa* 'Alba Semiplena'.

Or, as Shakespeare expressed it in "Sonnet 99," "The roses fearfully on thorns did stand, one blushing shame, another white despair...."

Both specimens have been planted in the Wars of the Roses Garden located on the east side of the grassy courtyard that encompasses the Shakespeare Gardens. Historically, Henry Tudor ultimately claimed the throne as heir of the House of Lancaster. But in contemporary Boulder, York is clearly the winner, to judge from the flourishing, head-high creamy white rosebush that eclipses its dark red neighbor, which is skimpier and has fewer flowers.

Marlene, who can quote Shakespeare's botanical lines at the drop of her gardening hat, isn't sure why the York rose has overtaken its Lancastrian cousin. She does have a theory,

Cupid's dart, a perennial, makes an appearance in the garden.

though, about the unexpected coloration of the neighboring Tudor rose, originally chosen by Henry VII to represent the new political alliance.

Rosa x *damascena*, also referred to as the damask rose, usually puts forth distinctive bicolor pink and white blooms rather than its current all-pinkish petals. "I've been doing a little research," Marlene notes. "People add different things to the soil to get different colors. There's something about this rose that requires something in the soil."

All three rose plants are what are called old-garden or heritage roses, plants that were in existence before 1867, the year that marks the introduction of the first cultivated hybrid tea rose. Fragrant old garden roses, the kind that would have perfumed Elizabethan yards, are very hardy, which makes them a good choice for Colorado's unpredictable climate.

Unlike many modern specimens, old garden roses only bloom once a year, usually in early June before the festival opens. Because most visitors arrive after the heritage flowers have faded, representative red and white roses—modern miniatures that bloom all summer—will be displayed in the Highlight Garden, which changes annually to focus on herbs and plants connected with each season's plays.

A hybrid rose by David Austin, also called an English rose.

EDIBLE HERBS CAST IN AN IMPORTANT ROLE

Nearby is the Long Garden, which displays roses with Shakespearean names, such as the red-purple Prospero and the peach-tinted Sweet Juliet. This bed also usually includes familiar staples such as the Madonna lily, cupid's darts, strawberries, lavender, and an aromatic rosemary shrub, planted afresh each season thanks to a donation from a local nursery.

Calendula flowers, with their bright saffron-colored blossoms, were mentioned in Shakespeare's works.

In addition to providing a fragrant ambience, the plants and herbs were also popular edibles in Shakespeare's time. The Bard, Marlene points out, would have eaten salads that contained dozens of herbs and colorful flowers, such as tiny pansies that dotted Elizabethan gardens more than four hundred years ago.

"The large pansies that we know have only been in cultivation about two hundred and fifty years," Marlene notes. "They were all developed from this little pansy," she says, pointing to delicate lavender and gold flowers perched on their stems like tiny butterflies. "Shakespeare called it love-in-idleness. We call them Johnny-jump-ups."

Occasionally, like actors reluctant to make their final exits, plants sometimes linger past their appointed time. Mary Hay, one of a half-dozen volunteers taking part in the weekly weeding and planting chores, points out a single leek that survived the winter. The pungent vegetable, here a spindly remnant, had its moment of glory in *Henry V* as the tempestuous officer Fluellen delivered a lively comedic bit sparked by lines such as, "If you can mock a leek, you can eat a leek."

As though trying to cheer the solitary leek with a colorful display, pink and white dianthus and orange calendula brighten the area, as do nearby baby carnations and a lush bed of wild thyme, the herb topped with tiny pink flowers.

One of the newest additions is the small Knot Garden. "I think we're famous," Marlene jokes, adding that at only a few feet long, this is surely the smallest knot garden in existence. Named for their curved, interlocking designs, the concept for the large geometric layouts was brought back from the Holy Land by the Crusaders. Knot gardens quickly became popular throughout the English countryside.

Traditionally, boxwood is used as a border for knot gardens. But the plant doesn't do well in Colorado. "As the soil freezes and thaws here over the winter, the roots come up, are exposed, and freeze," Marlene explains. So this knot garden instead has a border of *Teucrium,* a traditional Elizabethan plant that has delicate, feathery leaves.

THE BARD'S LIFE STILL OPEN TO INTERPRETATION

In addition to all his references to plants and herbs, Shakespeare also works in comments about trees in such plays as *As You Like It* which is set in the Forest of Arden. "Some of his commentary in *As You Like It,*" Mary points out, "is almost environmental, very applicable today."

Anyone familiar with the Bard's works is aware of his enormous knowledge about myriad subjects. With much about Shakespeare's life still open to interpretation, there has always been speculation about who—and what—he actually was.

"Lawyers thought he was a lawyer; he knew so much about law," Marlene says. "Doctors thought he must have been a doctor, sailors a sailor. Everybody claims Shakespeare for their own."

Including gardeners, who marvel at how much he reveals in his plays about plants, from their beauty to their poisonous properties. "Shakespeare knew a great amount," Marlene says. She's reminded of this every year, when Shakespeare Gardens group members gather to go over the festival's upcoming plays and discuss pertinent plants and quotations.

Small pansies were favorites in Elizabethan times.

"As gardeners," Marlene says, "we sit around the table and say: 'He's done it again.'"

Planting a Shakespearean Garden

Buttercup, Cuckow buds *(Ranunculus)*

Calendula *(Calendula officinalis)*

Chamomile *(Anthemis nobilis)*

Columbine *(Aquilegia vulgaris)*

Cowslip *(Primula veris)*

Fennel *(Foeniculum vulgare)*

Feverfew *(Matricaria eximia)*

Foxglove *(Digitalis purpurea)*

French Tarragon *(Artemisia dracunculus)*

Horehound *(Marrubium vulgare)*

Houseleek *(Sempervivum)*

Hyssop *(Hyssopus officinalis)*

Iris *(Pallida variegata)*

Lady's bedstraw *(Galium verum)*

Lady's Mantle *(Alchemilla mollis)*

Lavender *(Lavandula hidcote)*

Lemon balm *(Melissa officinalis)*

Little English Daisy *(Bellis perennis)*

Marjoram *(Origanum majorana)*

Nettle *(Lamium galeobdolon)*

Pansy *(Viola tricolor)*

Pennyroyal *(Mentha pulegium)*

Peppermint *(Mentha piperita)*

Pinks *(Dianthus allwoodii)*

Poet's narcissus *(Narcissus poeticus* var. *recurvus)*

Primrose *(Primula vulgaris)*

Red wild thyme *(Thymus serpyllum coccineus)*

Rosemary *(Rosmarinus prostrata)*

Rue *(Ruta graveolens)*

Santolina *(Santolina neopolitana)*

Strawberry *(Rosaceae)*

Sweet bay *(Laurus nobilis)*

Sweet woodruff *(Galium odoratum)*

Thyme *(Thymus vulgaris)*

RESOURCES

Colorado Shakespeare Festival, University of Colorado 277 UCB, Boulder, 80309; 303-492-0554; www.coloradoshakes.org. Information on the entire festival, including the gardens.

■ RECOMMENDED READING

Shakespeare's Flowers by Jessica Kerr, illustrated by Anne Ophelia Dowden (Johnson Books, 1997; reprinted from an earlier, out-of-print edition in the 1960s).

ORDINARY COMFORT:
BUNGALOWS AND COTTAGES

■ Be It Ever So Humble: The Colorado Craftsman and Bungalow

by NIKI HAYDEN

Architect Jim Marsden is checking the progress of his patient. It's an early–twentieth-century home facing surgery: a garage job plus a total family room and rear master bedroom lift. This modest family home has had years rolled back to reveal roots of a Colorado craftsman and bungalow style.

Materials, such as river rocks, bricks, woodwork, and built-in shelves, are hallmarks of craftsman and bungalow style homes.

Jim will tell you he had good bones to build upon. He admires the river-rock foundations, the wide front porch with tapered pillars. Added rooms may have turned a modest home into a larger, modern-day showpiece. But it's the materials and carpentry—river rocks, bricks, woodwork, and built-in shelves, that link this home to its humble origin.

"There's a hierarchy to these homes," he says. "At grade level you'll find a crude material. Then, the next level the materials are more refined—from rubble stone to a cut stone—then brick and wood. It's the same from front to back. You might find rubble stone in the back, but not in the front. You'll find siding in the front. But shingles, which are much cheaper, are in the back."

Colorado Craftsman Style Mingled with Victorian

California and New England Victorian homes were rolled out before the craftsman bungalows appeared. But in Colorado they were built side by side.

Stained glass windows are characteristic of the craftsman style.

That's because Colorado was settled much later than either the East or West Coast, which already had established Victorian neighborhoods. Originally, the craftsman bungalow may have been a reaction against the fussy, heavily ornamented Victorian style, although in Colorado, each mixed and mingled comfortably on the same street.

Victorian homes are vertical and narrow, often with pointed neo-Gothic arches. The bungalow contrasts by accenting horizontal lines. The difference is marked, yet each shares a common love for borrowed decorative details: a bit of Queen Anne for a Victorian, a slightly Japanese flavor to a craftsman bungalow.

Jim glances through a book on architecture and points to a Spanish bungalow with rounded arches or an English bungalow with Tudor trim. There's Frank Lloyd Wright's prairie school influence and the red tile and stone work of the Italian countryside, a style often referred to as Italianate. Jim's renovation looks all-American until you notice the roofline. And there it is—a slightly upturned flip that echoes a Chinese influence.

Origins of the Craftsman Bungalow

The architectural philosophy behind the American craftsman and bungalow styles can be traced to the nineteenth-century British arts and crafts movement made famous by William Morris. His artistic revolution championed handcrafted work as a reaction against the machine age of the Industrial Revolution.

The homeowners found light fixtures and furniture that keep the original style of the era.

Morris looked to previous ages, such as the medieval, for inspiration. He also looked to nature for forms and patterns, with stylized flowers, leaves, and stems appearing in many of the elements he designed for homes. Hand-blown glass, ironwork, carpentry, and hand letterpress books—the arts and crafts period celebrated modest rooms centered upon the hearth and a house filled with excellent carpentry. Built-in cabinets, simple oak furniture, uncluttered rooms, handcrafted iron hardware, and stained glass defined the look.

A comfortable chair and exquisite stained glass lamp reflect the handcrafted look that remains popular.

Ironically, Morris's intention to serve the working and middle classes unraveled when only the wealthy could afford his look. But the popular aesthetic sailed across the Atlantic Ocean and rooted in American soil.

At the same time, a simple beach home called the bungalow emigrated from India via colonial Brits to seaside resorts in England. The bungalow is defined as a one-and-a-half story home with a wide front porch and distinctive roof with overhanging eaves. As these modest homes popped up around the seaports of New England and the Atlantic states, they offered an opportunity for mail-order businesses. Between 1910 and 1920, Sears and Roebuck shipped many of the materials—primarily lumber and blueprints—out west via train. You had to hire your own carpenter, but a cost between $500 and $3,000 made the bungalow affordable and attractive to Colorado homebuyers. And locally manufactured bricks or quarried rocks completed the homes.

The large hearth was the centerpiece of a craftsman home.

The look of the craftsman style, with its love for rustic materials, rushed into an instant marriage with the bungalow. It was a perfect match.

A Look Men Love

The elegant whipped-cream-and-wedding-cake style of Victoriana is ultrafeminine, but men love the craftsman look. The attention to wooden joints, the stripped-bare but comfortable furniture, there's not a man who doesn't fall in love at first sight. "It's a lodge style by the lake,' Jim admits. "You know you'll just walk in, sit in a comfortable, ugly old chair, and have a drink and a smoke."

It's a home designed and built lovingly by a carpenter. Wood matters. It can't be painted or carved. Even if the wood is oak, it's often stained dark—all the better to dominate the interior. Stained glass windows replace the fussiness of curtains. A fire crackles in the hearth. Furniture, built from unpainted oak, is wide with comfortable cushions propped up against the wooden slats. Navajo rugs—handwoven, of course—grace the floor. Light fixtures fashioned from iron take on the medieval look with sturdy metal frames and hammered flourishes.

A simple yet elegant sturdy staircase shows off the lustrous character of wood.

Changing the Character of a Tract Home

For Robert and Katie Harberg, the craftsman style represents a nostalgic trip to their Nebraska roots. Katie grew up in a foursquare house with detailing in oak, a grand staircase, and wide porches. She says

A wood-paneled porch off the kitchen was added to the home. But fixtures and the style are in keeping with the original home.

midwestern homeowners indulge a love for their homes by prizing lovely interior detailing and lavish gardens. She has been influenced by that passion. "I can remember rows and rows of blooming iris among the gardens of the house behind us in Nebraska," she says, where elaborate perennial gardens were commonplace.

Robert and Katie's 1960s ranch tract house lacked character and amenities they wanted for their growing family. They considered moving to a larger home, but wanted to stay within range of the schools their kids attended.

"That meant the stock of houses available was limited," Robert says, "and the houses we looked at needed work. Most needed new kitchens and bathrooms. We'd been through that and knew how tough and expensive that was." But their real estate broker told them that houses are appraised according to square footage. Would it be worthwhile to put so much loving care into a small home?

Maybe. They carefully considered what was important to their family. "We thought this street could support a renovation." Katie says. Along the hilly street, nondescript homes have taken on face-lifts. Many of the neighbors may have come to the same conclusions as the Harbergs.

An architect friend suggested that Jim would "craftsman it up for them." Once they decided to make over the house, they set to work. The kitchen was expanded from the back of the garage, which gave them more room in the most heavily used space of the house. Robert chose cherry cabinets. That choice influenced all the wood trim in the dining and living rooms, which also is in cherry. They like the reddening and darkening that comes as cherry ages. Robert says that what men notice first in the house is the wood trim on the ceiling. He loves the symmetry of the style, the gleam of polished wood pillars and shelves.

There's a staircase with an arts and crafts style balustrade leading to the lower level. Wrought iron lamps give a soft glow, and their brick hearth will soon be tiled in a sage green. All throughout the house, the predominance of wood is a reminder of Robert's grandparents' house. His grandfather was in the lumber business, and he says the attention to woodwork in their home was exquisite.

Although the influence of Frank Lloyd Wright's prairie school was in greater abundance in their Nebraska towns, for their own home, Katie says that craftsman works best. It's small enough to convey a bungalow feel. Because the house was plain, they didn't have to take much away. They've simply added. What she loves about the craftsman style is the coziness, a rustic informality that always indicates the mark of the carpenter. Those are the same characteristics that made previous generations fall in love with the original bungalow.

A tract home is transformed into a craftsman home with an elaborate pergola.

A distinguished pergola with a slight Chinese influence creates a walkway from the street to the front door. Katie desperately wanted to change the exterior of her home. "We tried to deemphasize the garage and emphasize the front door," she says. The house no longer looks like tract architecture. It would be hard to imagine that it was anything but a craftsman home.

PASADENA: THE BUNGALOW CAPITAL

The bungalow capital of America isn't Colorado, but California. Robert says he'd like to tour the Gamble House in Pasadena—built for the millionaire Gamble of Proctor & Gamble in 1907. So much of the Harbergs' own house is a rediscovery of two great American architect brothers: Charles and Henry Greene. Originally based in Pasadena, California, the surviving Greene homes are celebrated and toured regularly. The Gamble House has become a museum

A garage and fencing are designed to reflect the original lines of the house.

preserved and managed by the University of Southern California.

From the 1950s to the 1980s, bulldozers erased bungalows for housing developments and high-rise buildings. By the 1990s, a movement emerged to protect and restore bungalows—elevating them to the status of a modest American classic.

The movement is so popular today that it's possible to buy furniture, lamps, windows, and doorknobs in the craftsman style. Sure, it's rare to find originals. Bungalow furniture was worn out. No one thought it might be valuable someday. When Barbra Streisand's

Today, reproduction tiles, furniture, lamps, and hardware are available for this popular style.

collection went on sale in 1999 at a New York auction house, it made the news. A New Jersey museum paid $125,000 for a pair of cabinets made by craftsman-style furniture makers, L & J. G. Stickley, Inc.

The venerable old firm of L. & J. G. Stickley, Inc., is still engaged in a brisk business. A lively competitor with Frank Lloyd Wright in his day, Gustav Stickley turned out the straightforward oak furniture so often photographed in craftsman houses.

If you'd like to re-create the craftsman and bungalow style today, there are plenty of resources. It's one of the easiest to reprise, whether it's the outside of your home or an interior. You'll find more books, architects, interior designers, and furniture makers devoted to this look than ever before.

RESOURCES

■ FURNITURE MAKERS

The Crafted Home, Steve Ciancio (designer), Denver; www.thecrafted home.com. Specializing in craftsman style.

Darrell Peart, Furnituremaker, 3419 C Street Northeast, No. 16, Auburn, Washington 98002; 425-277-4070; www.furnituremaker.com. Furniture made in style of Charles Greene and Henry Greene homes.

L. & J. G. Stickley, Inc., One Stickley Drive, Manlius, New York 13104; 315-682-5500; www.stickley.com. The original Stickley furniture that was so popular in bungalows.

■ HELPFUL ORGANIZATIONS

The Arts & Crafts Society, 1194 Bandera Drive, Ann Arbor, Michigan 48103; 734-358-6882; www.arts-crafts.com. Covers the history and literature of the period.

The Boettcher Mansion, in the Lookout Mountain Nature Preserve, 900 Colorow Road, Golden, 80401; 303-526-0855; http://ww2.co.jefferson.co.us/ext/dpt/comm_res/boettcher. An excellent example of the arts and crafts style from 1917. Also the headquarters of the Colorado Arts & Crafts Society.

Colorado Preservation, Inc., 1900 Wazee Street, Suite 360, Denver, 80202; 303-893-4260; www.coloradopreservation.org. Contains links to many Colorado historical websites.

Gamble House, 4 Westmoreland Place, Pasadena, California 91103; 626-793-3334; www.gamblehouse.org. This masterwork by Charles Greene and Henry Greene, the crown jewel of the craftsman bungalow design, is now a museum. Managed by the University of Southern California.

Historic Boulder, 646 Pearl Street, Boulder, 80302; 303-444-5192; www.historicboulder.org.

Historic Denver, 1536 Wynkoop Street, Suite 400A, Denver, 80202; 303-534-5288; www.historicdenver.org.

On-Line Arts & Crafts Movement Resource Directory; www.ragtime.org/index1.html. A Denver site devoted to the arts of the arts and crafts period.

■ PUBLICATIONS

American Bungalow Magazine, P.O. Box 756, 123 South Baldwin Avenue, Sierra Madre, California 91024; 800-350-3363; www.ambungalow.com.

Greene & Greene: Architecture as a Fine Art/Furniture and Related Designs by Randell L. Makinson (Gibbs Smith Publisher, 2001). This combined two-volume reissue is a definitive classic on the famous arts and crafts architects. It is written by the foremost expert on Greene & Greene, who has several other books on the subject.

■ EVERGREEN:
CONIFERS CREATE WINTER COMFORT

by NIKI HAYDEN

After perennials wither and autumn leaves litter the sidewalks, evergreens claim the landscape. We first notice the striking shapes—conical blue spruces, spherical piñon pines, mop-top ponderosas, creeping junipers, Christmas tree–shaped Douglas firs. It's only when we get to know them that we appreciate their hardiness.

"Where would we be without conifers?" asks Andrew Pierce, gardens director for Hudson Gardens in Littleton, during a winter walk through a pathway of evergreens.

The Conifer Grove is a semicircle of selected evergreens at the gardens. They form a mass that offers year-round shelter. "A curving road so that there's

A wide sweep tilts into a bowl that provides a slope, allowing water to run downhill.

always a surprise around the corner," Andrew says, "quite different from a formal design of straight paths where all is revealed."

We stop at a ponderosa pine next to an Austrian pine. The Austrian is an introduced pine species from Europe close in appearance to the ponderosa and with similar growing habits. "The Austrian is a little greener," Andrew says and then compares the needles of the two trees. The ponderosa needle is nearly four times longer and once provided the weft for Native American basket weaving.

The ponderosa's brown needles drift down, settling on limbs. All evergreens shed their needles—every three years for the ponderosa—as a form

Pine needles shed every three years on a ponderosa pine.

of rejuvenation. "I've been getting quite a few calls lately. People have been seeing the brown needles accumulating and think there is something wrong with their trees. But it's quite natural," Andrew says.

Conifers Are Ancient, Remarkable

Conifers—cone-bearing trees and shrubs—include evergreens, although strictly speaking, not all evergreens are conifers. And a few conifers, like the larch, actually lose their leaves. Most conifers that are evergreens grow thin needles that do not desiccate and will carry the plant through a tough winter.

Conifers are hardy, durable plants and among the longest lived. The redwood tree is one example. "And to see the size of the seed of the redwood. It's quite amazing that such an enormous tree could come from such a tiny seed," Andrew says. Bristlecone pines on Mount Evans are more than one thousand years old. Andrew recalls one bristlecone variety in Arizona believed to be more than four thousand years old.

But that's not the only amazing fact about conifers. They often grow in bands at different mountain altitudes—a lodgepole pine rarely grows under an elevation of eight thousand feet. Ponderosas spread out, never touching each other, while lodgepoles grow densely.

Ponderosa pines will grow on the dry side of a mountain; Douglas firs spread across the damper area, each suited to the sun exposure and snow runoff of a mountainside. Unlike deciduous trees, large drifts of snow rarely break or injure the branches of conifers, a perfection of botanical design in mountain settings.

That's why you won't find them native to the plains of Colorado. "Denver is a planted city," Andrew says as he looks west to the Rockies. "There's no native conifer until you reach the foothills. There's only one exception to this and that's the Black Forest in Parker. There, conifers grow in sand rather than the granite of the mountains. Perhaps they're a remnant of an ancient forest that once covered Colorado."

PLANTING CONIFERS

The conifers at Hudson Gardens are planted on high ground, surrounding a sweeping lawn tilting into a bowl of green pasture. The designer chose this site because conifers require excellent drainage. After all, most originate on mountainsides where water runs downhill and never lingers.

Not all the trees along this wide sweep have the same needs, but those of like requirements are grouped together appropriately. Piñon pines are from southwestern Colorado where rainfall is scant. The Colorado blue spruce like medium watering, so they're grouped where water will stand a bit longer. Junipers will thrive with little water. Here they receive far less than a lawn or garden requires.

To plant conifers, Andrew suggests buying a tree between six and twelve feet in height. Plant it in a hole about one foot wider than the root ball. He adds a small amount of compost but no more than one-fifth of all the soil. Water well as the dirt is pushed back into the hole; fill all the pockets and water as you go. A transplant will require a bit more water the first year, but don't flood the plant. It's best planted away from lawn or perennials so that the tree is not overwatered.

Fill in the hole so that the soil at the trunk is about two inches above the soil line.

The conifer walk at Hudson Gardens is designed in a circle to reveal the vista slowly.

This allows water to run away from the trunk of the tree. Water then may pool in a depression of soil where the new tips of roots are growing. The best time for planting is April or early May.

Avoid Pruning, Consider Smaller Varieties

Healthy specimens rarely harbor disease and require little care. "We don't prune and there's no reason to spray," Andrew says. "We have a slight aphid infestation on the spruce, but it's of no consequence and does no damage other than cosmetic."

Even junipers add to winter interest. Many have been overplanted along the Front Range and heavily pruned as foundation plantings. Crowding

Native junipers, often harshly pruned, have a beautiful shape of their own.

diminishes these drought-tolerant shrubs, and pruning shortens their life span. If allowed their own space, they form a bridge between the low-growing dwarf pines and taller species. In the Conifer Grove, a 'Wichita Blue' juniper adds a bluish tint to a green forest.

"There's a lot of white in the blue spruce and blue junipers," Andrew says as he holds on to a prickly spruce limb. "That's what gives it a blue color."

A tabletop juniper, dwarf mugo pine, and a dwarf Norway spruce provide smaller collections close to the path. Andrew says the biggest mistake home gardeners make when they plant conifers is to choose a tree that will grow too large. Perhaps it's close to the house or takes over a small lawn. Suddenly a magnificent tree has grown out of proportion to its surroundings.

Andrew says that a western white fir, set among the medium-size trees, is lovely, and should be considered. It offers a more petite size and softer shape than most conifers, with wispy, delicate needles and a stunning trunk. "Firs are soft," Andrew says, holding a feathery branch, "spruces are prickly." Consider the newer, smaller conifers. With so many dwarf varieties today, such as the dwarf Norway spruce, evergreens can thrive for many years, even in small gardens.

THE HUDSON GARDENS CONIFER GROVE

FOUNDATION CONIFERS

Austrian pine *(Pinus nigra)*
Colorado blue spruce *(Picea pungens)*
Ponderosa pine (*Pinus ponderosa* spp. *scopulorum)*

ADDITIONAL TREES AND SHRUBS

'Burkii' juniper (*Juniperus virginiana* 'Burkii')
Cologreen juniper (*Juniperus scopulorum* 'Cologreen')
Douglas fir *(Pseudotsuga menziesii)*
Dwarf mugo pine *(Pinus mugo pumilio)*
Gray gleam juniper (*Juniperus scopulorum* 'Gray Gleam')
Limber pine *(Pinus flexilis)*
White fir *(Abies concolor)*

RESOURCES

Arapahoe Acres Nursery, 9010 South Santa Fe Drive, Littleton, 80125; 303-791-1660; www.arapahoeacres.com.

Colorado State University Nursery and Conservation Tree Planting Program, 3843 Laporte Avenue, Fort Collins, 80523; 970-491-6303 (Colorado State Forest Service).

Cherry Creek Tree Farms, 15290 East Arapahoe Road, Aurora, 80016; 303-690-8733; www.cherrycreektreefarms.com.

Fort Collins Nursery, 2121 East Mulberry, Fort Collins, 80524; 970-482-1984; www.fortcollinsnursery.com.

Hudson Gardens, 6115 South Santa Fe Drive, Littleton, 80120; 303-797-8565; www.hudsongardens.org.

Paulino Gardens, 6300 North Broadway, Denver, 80216; 303-429-8062; www.paulinogardens.com.

Tagawa Garden Center, 7711 South Parker Road, Aurora, 80016; 303-690-4722; www.tagawagardens.com.

Timberline Gardens, 11700 West 58th Avenue, Arvada, 80004; 303-420-4060; www.timberlinegardens.com. Also has unique drought-tolerant plants.

Treehouse Nursery, 7450 Valmont Road, Boulder, 80301; 303-449-8733.

The Tree Farm, 11868 Mineral Road (Highway 52), Longmont, 80504; 303-652-2961.

Wilmore Nursery, Garden Center & Greenhouse, 711 East County Road, Littleton, 80122; 303-795-5339; www.wilmorenurseries.com.

■ THE COLORADO COTTAGE: LIVING LARGE IN A SMALL SPACE

by NIKI HAYDEN

"My house and garden, together, are the size of your thumb," says Lawrie Diack Wilson about her 1,200-square-foot cottage and surrounding garden. As individual as a thumbprint, as intimate as the palm of her hand, Lawrie's home is a patch of whimsy, a storybook setting on a handkerchief-size plot of land.

Twenty-two years ago, when Lawrie spent a year looking for a house she could afford, she knew that restoring a turn-of-the-century cottage was right for her. Even before the popular trend in country and cottage homes, Lawrie imagined herself designing a garden that would surround and embellish a small cottage.

"I knew I wanted to restore an old house, but I had no time, money, or talent. I don't know why I thought I could do it," she says, as an encouraging word to others who may feel as hapless. Today, Lawrie's 1906 cottage looks like an illustration in a book of children's verses: a vine-covered dwelling smothered in heirloom blooms. But like all home renovations, the beginning efforts were jolting.

Lawrie's turn-of-the-century cottage is in character with heirloom flowers and old-fashioned fruit trees.

"I started with the electrical work and electrocuted myself three times. Then I turned to the wallpaper and it all rolled off the walls. It was the kind of house that if you tried to make toast and operate the oven, you would blow a fuse. And the structural engineer I hired to look it over told me it would

A cottage festooned with vines and flowers is a backdrop for birdhouses and whimsical statuary.

never fall down, but I'd freeze to death. I guess that's why they had three wood-burning stoves," she says.

It's all grist for the usual stories about renovation. While Lawrie has received offers to buy the house, she wouldn't think of moving. "All that I've put into this home," she says, "I couldn't leave."

Although Lawrie's house is almost one hundred years old, she's only the third owner. A stucco-covered brick cottage, it has an ample front porch, small living room, dining room, kitchen, two bedrooms, one bathroom, and a tiny closed-in porch. It's far removed from the large and imposing current-day homes, but Lawrie loves the small spaces, historic touches of built-in cabinets and shelves, and the patina only time can create. "I always wanted a comfortable, cozy, romantic cottage," she says, much like a bird's nest perched in a large, sturdy tree: a home that serves as a buffer against the turmoil of the world outside.

A Palette from the Rose Family

Open the front door to Lawrie's home and it's unabashedly personal, like looking inside a woman's jewelry box. The colors are red: deep wine, pastel pinks, rose and scarlet. "I love red. I love cranberry, merlot, and raspberry. Red is an easy color to work with," she says, with a wave of her hand to embrace all the shades, hues, values of the rose family. Not many designers would agree. Red is a hot color, determined and powerful. But

The home's reds were inspired by Chinese figurines.

Lawrie's mix of reds reflects the gleam of old wood that frames doors, windows and cabinets. In a house that could be dark and cold, red radiates warmth.

Red simply slipped in when Lawrie wanted to show off a few old porcelain Chinese figurines with red-lacquer touches. Red complemented her Chinese-influenced furniture. By then, the color won her over: the windows are draped in red toile; the small couch is a wine damask. Comfortable chairs are speckled in red and white stripes. Even the laundry room is lined in pink and white gingham wallpaper. The tiny closed-in porch is painted shell pink. Pink sandals are poised outside the front door.

Perhaps most surprising is the marble countertop in the kitchen. It's a rosy hue, with streaks of yellow and gray. "Everyone warned me about marble," Lawrie says, "but I love it. I love the colors. I'd been to Italy and saw marble hundreds of years old. It still looked good to me. I'm careful not to cut on it, but it looks good today."

Comfortable furniture is accented by Chinese pottery.

CREATIVE WAYS TO FIND SPACE

The kitchen is Lawrie's only nod to modern touches. Originally it was small, windowless, and grimy. A wall that served as a hallway was removed, a skylight added to provide natural light. The kitchen turned into a study of more for less. New cabinets reach to the ceiling—a sure way to provide more storage for a small room. Brass rods along one wall hold a copper cookie cutter collection. It could also hold pots and pans, she points out. A built-in ironing board cupboard is revamped. Every nook and cranny was put to practical use; the real trick was to find appliances that would fit into small spaces. After nine layers of linoleum, she uncovered a pristine wood floor that had never been walked on.

Like all renovations, the job took months. "Of course, we had margaritas and Triscuits every night for dinner during all that renovation. There was nothing to cook with," she says with a sigh.

Then she turned toward the one bathroom. Since Lawrie wanted to go back in time, she decided to get rid of the standard bathtub and replace it with

A tiny kitchen is made more spacious by spare lines.

a claw-foot tub. "You can find them in varying lengths, but generally only one width. I discovered that with that width, we wouldn't have been able to close the bathroom door. That's the kind of thing I would have done in the beginning—buy a bathtub too wide for the door to close." Eventually, with luck and persistence, Lawrie did locate a narrower tub.

She also discovered techniques, through trial and error, to expand on cramped areas: "A few inches can make a difference in a small space," she says. Just taking off the footboard of her bed opened more space. Choosing a small two-seater couch fits the living room without swallowing it. A few comfortable chairs serve her needs. But she didn't give up her ample Chinese dining table that easily seats a crowd. And she has sprinkled antique chests and tables judiciously throughout her home, none oversized.

Keeping to one color, rich and varied in hue, helps to unify a small space. But within those strictures, Lawrie has decided to be dramatic. The bedroom walls are covered in enormous pink blossoms. The textiles chosen for the beds and windows are floral—a continuing theme, but not the same pattern. "I like

A Wardian case from Victorian times holds a collection of shells.

color on color, texture on texture, and luscious fabrics," Lawrie says, and in keeping the bedroom furniture small, the patterns dominate space rather than objects.

ORIGINAL OR REPRODUCTION?

Lawrie's house is landmarked with her local historic society. But that doesn't mean that everything in the house dates to 1906. She had to decide what was most important to be original and what could be reproduction. Lighting fell into the category of reproduction. She discovered that even reproduction lamps could be tricky to install and decided to seek an expert. Old homes are especially difficult to run wire through because of crumbling plaster. It's important, she notes, to find an electrician who is familiar with the problems of old houses. Today, rose-colored shades glow in a burgundy dining room and above the original salt-glazed brick fireplace.

An vy-covered cottage with potted geraniums and a wide porch—a lavish garden on a small scale.

The closet doors with leaded glass panes came from the original kitchen of the house. Whenever possible, Lawrie saved original cabinets, pieces of wood, and bits of hardware. You'll never know when they may come in handy, even if it's decades later. After twenty years, she's not quite finished. There's a small basement where a guest bedroom is being renovated.

And a closed attic upstairs will need attention soon. Lawrie imagines a winding staircase to a room upstairs. It will take time, and she will start slowly.

"Sometimes I make mistakes and it looks awful. Then I have to adapt," she says, knowing what she wants the end result to be: "To come home to a small space after the crush of the day. Just to open the front door and walk inside— it feels serene." Renovating her home is only half the picture. From the very beginning, Lawrie designed a cottage garden as remarkable as filigree around a small gem.

RESOURCES

■ VICTORIANA COUNTRY ACCESSORIES

Different Drummer Antiques, 5465 Manhart Street, Sedalia, 80135; 303-688-0133.

Sharon's, 315 Mountain Avenue, Berthoud, 80513; 970-532-7071.

Painted Primrose, 149 B Second Avenue, Niwot, 80544; 303-652-0525.

■ MARBLE COUNTERTOPS

Colorado Stone Company, 1635 North Main Street, Longmont, 80501; 303-776-0674.

■ SUMMER'S LAST HURRAH:
A COTTAGE GARDEN TO END THE SEASON

by NIKI HAYDEN

Most garden tours take place in June when the grand perennials make their entry. The roses are flush with bloom. Delphiniums stand tall and straight. Poppies wave with brilliant color. So it's unusual to find a gardener who sweeps all aside to concentrate on a late summer show. But Lawrie Diack Wilson does just that.

She's a landscape designer whose business is frantic from April to July. By August, it's winding down. That's when she has a chance to take a breath and immerse herself in her own cottage garden, which is most spectacular from August through September. While there are plenty of annuals like cosmos for bold blooms, Lawrie first designed her late summer garden with a single thought: semidwarf fruit trees.

"I started with the orchard. A standard apple tree," she says. "I didn't know the difference between a standard and dwarf at the time." But Lawrie knew she wanted a cottage garden. Her 1906 bungalow on a small lot offered a wide porch, built-in cabinets, wood trim, and turn-of-the-century charm. Filled with antique velvet

A grape arbor stretches over the walkway to Lawrie's cottage. By September, the arbor exudes the scent of grape jelly.

loveseats, pink and gold china, leaded glass cabinets—the landmarked house is carefully preserved. But outside, a patchy lawn and large street-side tree were the only plantings. Lawrie converted her tiny lawn into an extravagant old-fashioned garden and planted ivy that quickly covered the cottage.

THE DEFINING CHARACTERISTICS OF A COTTAGE GARDEN

"I think of a cottage garden as having boundaries: it may be a low fence, like a picket fence, or hedges," Lawrie says. "And then it will have some whimsical ornamentation—birdhouses, a gazing ball, or a bird bath. The plants include heirlooms, which are just old-fashioned varieties, and a gate or pergola covered in vines. I have grapes, clematis, and roses. And then there's a profusion of flower shapes: buttons, spikes, spires, plumes, umbels, daisies. It has a wild, unruly look."

Lawrie amid daylilies and coreopsis. A mix of flowers, shrubs, and trees, her garden doesn't have a scrap of grass.

Color is the hallmark of a cottage garden, Lawrie says, as she bends toward a velvety magenta daylily. The deep red is surrounded by bright yellow coreopsis. Silvery artemisia, lamb's ear, and santolina serve to bridge the expanses of green and bright color.

A dozen dwarf conifers, some in pots, are strewn throughout the garden. Like the dwarf fruit trees, they are kept in small scale. "Some I keep for a few years and then move," she says. But the fruit trees remain, gently arching, laden with tiny pears, cherries, peaches, plums, apples, or apricots. In one corner, Lawrie has stretched the limbs to form a canopy over two yellow wicker chairs. "You get blossoms in the spring, fruit in the summer, and color in the fall," she says about her fruit trees. "I don't know what else you could ask for." One apple variety dates back to the days of Isaac Newton. Perhaps it's the species of tree he sat under when the fabled apple fell, sparking his discovery of the law of gravity.

The trees are not without problems. The apple trees lost their blossoms when a late May storm hit. It wasn't the storm night that proved so fateful, but the two nights of intense cold that followed. "Usually, I'm out here in my pajamas trying to cover up the trees," she says, but it was useless. To ensure survival, her trees are custom designed: an heirloom apple is grafted onto a root of Siberian stock. The roots may survive temperatures of twenty below zero in a dire winter. In a warm spring the tree will give heirloom fruit, but not after a cold spring nips the buds. The fruit that weathers a Colorado spring is tiny and perfect, more decorative than edible.

Two small, fuzzy peaches are more decorative than edible.

HEALING GARDENS

Lawrie planted a delicate peach tree now festooned with tiny, fuzzy, rosy

A profusion of late summer bloom includes orange daylilies, white Queen Anne's lace, and rose of Sharon.

peaches in honor of her oncologist who treated her for breast cancer nearly a decade ago. "He was a special person," she says. "After a year of treatment I was laid off as an R.N. at the hospital. I was exhausted from the treatment and heartbroken to lose a job I loved. The doctors, nurses, and friends helped me survive. But my garden, in time, healed me. I truly believe that."

Cottage gardens first began as gardens for healing as well as subsistence. Dating back to Shakespeare's day, cottage gardens took hold when large English manors lost workers to the bubonic plague. As an enticement to the depleted labor force, lords and ladies allowed their farm helpers to set up cottages and coax plants of their own, rather than rely on the manor largesse.

Vivid orange daylilies are paired with silvery *Artemisia*.

Besides the usual vegetables, cottagers planted medicinal and culinary herbs. So many of our ornamental flowers planted today, such as rose hips containing vitamin C, once were cultivated as medicine. On the smallest sliver of land, English cottagers packed plants closely for the most efficient harvest. That unruly look is what gardeners enjoy today. No broad lawn; no thick tree trunks.

Lawrie enrolled in the master gardener program at Colorado State University, met Richard Elvins at Denver's Paulino Gardens (their plant propagator), and set up her own business. All the while, she was removing sod, laying down flagstone, planting trees, and covering her orchard floor with eight varieties of creeping thyme.

On a hot August morning, her business partner, Adrian Mondello, cuts flagstone to fit a pathway. His red wheelbarrow filled with stone is a reminder to passersby that a cottage garden requires intensive maintenance. That, Lawrie says, is a drawback for some gardeners. But not for her.

INTENSIVE GARDENING FOR A SMALL SPACE

"I love the work. You wouldn't believe the amount of soil amendments I've brought in. That's because a cottage garden is so thickly planted. And this year I added cocoa shell husks for mulch. Some smart

Small birdhouses hang from fruit tree limbs.

folks in Hershey, Pennsylvania, sell it. It smells chocolatey and is lovely to work in. And I irrigate by hand. Overall, I use much less water that way. There's always something to do. The downside is that sometimes it looks like an unmade bed."

August brings the hot colors: a red hibiscus, blue mist spiraea covered with bees, purple asters, and yellow cosmos. There are a few "weeds" that are cultivated: Queen Anne's lace and Maximilian's sunflowers. The thyme under the fruit trees is taking too long to spread, Lawrie laments, but the aroma of their crushed leaves wafts upward.

These heirloom plants are aromatic— like the thyme varieties underfoot. They remind us that so many hybrids today have had scent bred out of them. Flowers and shrubs are covered with bees and butterflies because many of the plants chosen for a cottage garden are rich in nectar. And the heirlooms take on a meadow appearance since many were originally wildflowers. They're tough plants from hardy stock.

The traditional rose of Sharon is a late summer bloomer.

A cottage garden is sensual: splashy color, the sounds of buzzing insects, and the perfume of bloom.

Finally, we end at the pergola, which serves as a welcoming gate to the flagstone path. Concord and Interlocken grapevines shade the arbor for 'Comtesse de Bouchaud' and 'Hagley' hybrid clematis. The grapevines are vigorous as tendrils spread along the fence. But there's another reason why Lawrie planted the grapes. In August and September, when the grapes are ripening, she says, "you can stand under this arbor and it smells like grape jam."

LAWRIE DIACK WILSON'S FLOWERS AND SEMIDWARF FRUIT TREES

Alcea rosea, also *rugosa* and *ficifolia:* all hollyhocks

Artemisia: eight varieties

Asclepias tuberosa: butterfly weed

Asters: eight varieties

Cosmos: 'Psyche', 'Seashell', 'Bright Lights', 'Ladybird', 'Hinumaru', 'Daydream', 'Purity', 'Pied Piper', 'Yellow Garden', 'Dazzler', 'Sensation', 'Versailles'

Echinops: blue globe thistle

Helianthus: *maximilianiis*

Hemerocallis fulva: common daylily

Hibiscus syriacus: rose of Sharon 'Minerva'

Liatris: gayfeather

Monarda: bee balm

Nepeta: catmint

Origanum laevigatum: 'Herrenhausen' oregano

Persicaria: firetails

Phlox: 'David's Summer White'

Physostegia: obedient plant

Roses, all with rugosa in their parentage: 'William Baffin', 'Buffalo Gal', 'Grootndorst', 'Hansa', 'Persian', 'Roselina', 'Thomas Lipton', 'Therese Bugnet', red leaf rose, Victorian rose

Rudbeckia: black-eyed Susan

Salvia azurea grandiflora: Azure sage

Salvia farinacea: 'Mealy Cup' sage

Salvia superba: 'May Night' sage

Santolina: lavender cotton

Scabiosa: pincushion flower

Sedum: autumn joy

Sidalcea: 'Elsie Heugh'

Stachys: lamb's ears

Thyme: eight varieties, 'Red Mother' and 'Lime' are favorites

ORCHARD TREES

Apple: red, golden, whitewinter Permian

Apricot: sungold and Manchurian

Cherry: northstar, Bing, Van

Peach: reliance, Siberian

Pear: D'anjou and Bartlett

Plum: Stanley and Santa Rosa

RESOURCES

■ ART GALLERIES CARRYING GARDEN-THEMED ART

Mary Williams Fine Arts, 2116 Pearl Street, Unit C, Boulder 80302; 303-938-1588;
www.marywilliamsfinearts.com.

Tam O'Neill Fine Art, 311 Detroit Street, Denver, 80206; 303-355-7777;
www.tamoneillfinearts.com.

■ SHOPS CARRYING COTTAGE GARDEN ITEMS

Birdsall & Co., 1540 South Broadway, Denver, 80210; 303-722-2535; www.birdsallgarden.com.

City Floral Greenhouse and Garden Center, 1440 Hearney, Denver, 80220; 303-399-1177;
www.cityfloralgreenhouse.com. Specialty is indoor potted plants.

HMK Designs, 312 University Boulevard, Denver, 80206; 303-321-5278. Custom dried flowers.

Indochine, 2525 Arapahoe Avenue, No. 31, Boulder, 80302; 303-441-7734. Glazed pots from
Southeast Asia.

L&M Garden Center, 735 East Colorado Highway 56, Berthoud, 80513; 970-532-3232;
www.lmgardencenter.com.

Rabbit Shadow Farm, 2880 East Highway 402, Loveland, 80537; 970-667-5531. Unusual topiary

of herbs and indoor plants, such as lavender and coleus. Workshops on topiary techniques.

Smith & Hawken, 268 Detroit Street, Denver, 80206; 303-329-6938; www.smithandhawken.com.

Sturtz & Copeland Florist & Greenhouse, 2851 Valmont Road, Boulder, 80301; 303-442-6663;

www.sturtzandcopelandflorist.com. Glazed and earth pots.

West End Gardener, 777 Pearl Street, Boulder, 80302; 303-938-0607.

ATOMIC-AGE CLASSICS:

COLORADO MODERNISM

■ THE MODERN TOUCH: A MODERNIST HOME AS GALLERY AND LIBRARY

by NIKI HAYDEN

When Helen and Robert Davis designed a house in 1969, they relied upon twentieth-century modernism—architecture defined by a spare space of elemental shapes and clean lines.

Helen is an artist. It's not surprising that she looked to modernism for her home. With the 1950s and 1960s behind her, she valued the strong, pure lines of modern design but wanted to shape her own aesthetic. "Some of the modernist houses had low ceilings. I wanted light and space," she says. No dark halls. No tiny, clustered rooms. Sleek, open, uncluttered. Style, not size, mattered.

Both Robert and Helen collect art and books. They needed large white walls, high ceilings, and light-filled rooms with plenty of space for bookshelves and Helen's paintings. They ended up with an art gallery and library intimately arranged into a space they call home.

EMBRACING MODERNISM AS IT IS FADING

The Davis home was constructed late in the modernist period, but showcases the essential elements that set it apart from the past and the future. At a time when modernism was dwindling, the Davises embraced it.

In the decade of the 1950s, when war-weary Americans yearned for hearth and

The Davis home embraces the clean lines and simple geometric shapes that define modernist architecture.

home, some returned to the familiar bungalow.

But others, caught up in the legacy of Frank Lloyd Wright and the European immigrant Bauhaus designers, longed for a new bold design that cast aside familiar architecture. Strong geometric shapes did away with ornament and fuss. The sudden construction spurt in both the United States and Europe required striking buildings.

A long hall becomes a gallery and library.

Today, many of those structures look dated. Too utilitarian for some, too sterile for others, the modern movement deteriorated into big box stores and strip mall conventionality. In its best days, modernism streamlined everyday living by allowing simplicity and elegant shapes to dominate space in the same way that fine woodworking defined the arts and crafts movement. The best of the modernists is easy to point out. It remains beautiful still.

BREAKING RULES

Every room, every choice of wood, flooring, carpet, glass, has been carefully considered in the Davis home. Rather than sitting on a bulldozed plot, the house has been nestled into the soil. Windows fill half a wall or line an entire wall. Proportions are given consideration; scale is essential. There's no ostentation, ornament, or silliness. Everything matters, from the shape of a door to the placement of a kitchen cabinet. It's modern, but not cold, because its modest size encourages intimate spaces.

The white walls and neutral colors allow riotous color of art on walls and shelves to be showcased.

True to modernism, rules are meant to be broken. Instead of a large open porch, the front is private and closed off to the busy street outside, but windows in back face a heavily wooded canyon. Cabinets are flush, no knobs to break the lines. Colors are black, white, natural wood, or neutral tile. Furniture and carpeting are neutral, too. On the walls, color is riotous in the prints, paintings, folk art, pottery, and textiles. Iroquois masks mingle with color copier images. Textiles from Latin America float next to brightly patterned paintings. The bedroom is lined with prints, many from artist friends. Helen's series of painted hearts fills the front entry. Like the pottery that Robert and Helen collect, the house is a clean and perfect vessel to hold something precious.

In the 1960s, Helen chose the late L. Gale Abels as the architect, a former student of the great Finnish architect Eero Saarinen. Gale also had worked in the office of Walter Gropius, the Bauhaus émigré who taught at Harvard. "I made a book of certain things I liked and wanted," Helen says. "I don't think Gale read it. The first design he gave me was god-awful: all triangular rooms. I think he thought he had an artist and could be adventurous." Gale and Helen grappled with designing and redesigning, eventually settling on the current house. It has not changed since those original ideas. Not the kitchen, not the bathrooms. "I couldn't afford to make changes along the way," Helen says, and she is grateful that Gale's final plans were never altered.

FITTING IN

As the construction began, she simply had to sell her idea to the neighbors. After all, the surrounding homes are bungalows and Victorians—the antithesis of what Helen and Robert's home would represent. "I just knocked on the doors, took a bottle of wine, and celebrated with them,' she remembers, and was welcomed to the neighborhood. The Davises did make one concession: their home has a flat roof so as not to obstruct the view of their neighbors, who wanted to see the mountains in this foothills community.

"Of course, in this climate you should never build a flat roof," Helen says. "We could have tipped it a bit. But we've only had to shovel snow off once, so I shouldn't complain. It was the first house built in our community in thirty years. Some thought we were building a medical building, because of the roof and square, windowless front. But we all became good friends."

Modernist furniture, glass, dinnerware, and textiles may be making a revival, but Helen isn't so sure about homes. Contemporary houses are much larger than those of the 1950s and 1960s, and she wonders if homes of her era will survive intact. They aren't old enough to have the cachet of a Victorian, but they're too dated for our large-scale tastes.

SMALL SCALE

In the 1950s and 1960s, size alone wasn't the major criterion it is today. "It had to have city utilities, not be built on bentonite (a clay soil that shifts over time), and not be in a wind zone," she says. But one additional value stood out for her. "Modern can be claustrophobic. My husband

Collections of pottery feature ceramic artists the Davises have known.

Their kitchen is spare in mahogany wood and dark colors. Says Helen, "It all goes back to a feeling of space."

likes enclosed spaces, but I have to see the world. All the doorways and windows are eight feet high. That was my idea; I wanted a feeling of space. Today, I would want them nine or ten feet high."

Although Helen's home is only 1,734 square feet for each floor, it feels spacious. The living room is a perfect white cube with wood paneling that lines and borders the ceiling on one side like the lid on a box.

The sleek kitchen incorporates mahogany cabinets—costly today but reasonable back then. Helen daringly took her appliances to an auto shop to be painted black: "They couldn't believe anyone would paint a refrigerator black, so they painted everything midnight blue." The black, white, and mahogany tones set the stage for earthenware pottery—the only items on display.

Robert built their large dining table from a bowling alley. The discarded alley has been cut into an oval, sanded, and sealed. It's surrounded by black chairs and sits on a black pedestal. Robert also built the sculpture stands, bookcases, and storage cabinets throughout the house.

A House Designed for All Ages

Helen points out that her home is designed for low maintenance. There's no lawn to mow. The living spaces are one story. Her only regret is that the bathrooms would have to be remodeled for wheelchairs. "But maybe we won't need them," she says. "We thought about everything else for aging."

Flanked by a wall of windows that leads to a series of decks outside the sliding glass doors, a magnificent maple in a neighbor's yard spreads giant limbs for dense shade. Lilacs and an aromatic mock orange shrub stand like sentinels in a backyard that has no lawn and drops steeply to a small river canyon.

The sloping bank is covered in the native shrub Oregon grape, and a winding path and stairs lead down to the trickle of a river. "The front of the house is city," Helen says, "but the back is country. We can sit out here and feel like we are far away from city noises, even though the road out front is heavily used."

Since Helen and Robert's home appeared, a few other modernist homes have been built in the neighborhood. Rather than a jumble, the street is a study in styles: a bungalow cottage next to a white cube adjacent to a Victorian and Italianate. What allows this free mix is the scale of the homes. No one tried to fit a large home onto a small lot, or attach a huge wing onto a small house. They've kept to a consistency in the size of house and position on the lot.

Over time, the landscaping has knitted friends, neighbors, and architecture into a blended tapestry on a single theme of twentieth-century American architecture. But it was Helen and Robert who took that first chance that a modernist home could fit in and add charm without leading to disruption. "It's been mistaken for the garage of the house next door," Helen says with pride. Unobtrusive. Private. Modest. Some of the best elements of architecture are a whisper rather than a shout.

Nearly all the windows look out the back, where a wooded slope creates privacy. "The front of the house is city," Helen says, "the back is country."

RESOURCES

■ ACCURATE REPLACEMENT PARTS

A & A Tradin Post (an Ace Hardware), 4509 South Broadway, Englewood, 80110; 303-761-0747.

■ CONTEMPORARY INTERPRETATIONS

The Lighting Studio, 1024 Cherokee Street, Denver, 80204; 303-595-0900. Lighting fixtures, lamps, etc.

■ MUSEUMS

Denver Art Museum, 100 West 14th Avenue Parkway, Denver, 80204; 720-865-5000; www.denverartmuseum.org. An excellent design wing devoted to early modern and contemporary design.

National Center for Atmospheric Research, 1850 Table Mesa Drive, Boulder, 80305; 303-497-1000; www.ncar.ucar.edu/ncar/visitucar.html. Not strictly a museum, but worth seeing this world-class building designed by I. M. Pei; guided tours.

Vance Kirkland Museum and Foundation, 1311 Pearl Street, Denver, 80203; 303-832-8576; www.vancekirkland.org.

■ ORIGINAL FURNITURE, FURNISHINGS, AND OTHER DECORATIVE ITEMS

Crown Mercantile, 46 Broadway, Denver, 80203; 303-713-9593; www.crownmercantile.com. Also offers some reproductions and interpretations of decorative items.

Decade, 56 South Broadway, Denver, 80209; 303-733-2288. Also offers some reproductions and interpretations of decorative items and clothing.

Modern Classics, 1388 South Broadway, Denver, 80210 303-744-8999. Original furniture and furnishings; also offers reproductions of original furniture designs.

MOD Livin', 5327 East Colfax Avenue, Denver, 80220; 720-941-9292. Huge selection of original mid-century furniture, furnishings, decorative items, clothing.

One Home 1036 Speer Boulevard, Denver, 80204; 720-946-1505. Original furniture and furnishings.

Popular Culture, 1150 South Broadway, Denver, 80210; 303-777-1163. Original furniture, furnishings, decorative items.

Wazee Deco, 383 South Corona Street, Denver, 80218; 303-293-2144; www.wazeedeco.com. Original furniture, furnishings, decorative items.

■ SALVAGE SUPPLIERS

Do-It-Ur-Self Plumbing & Heating Supply, 3120 Brighton Boulevard, Denver, 80216; 303-297-0455.

Garrett Lumber & Wrecking Co., 7360 Grape Street, Commerce City, 80022; 303-288-4946 (office), 303-288-5932 (yard).

■ Rock Gardens: Laboratories of the World's Highest Places

by NIKI HAYDEN

Flip through the pages of horticulture history in the twentieth century and you'll see a parade of newfangled plants: elegant hybrid tea roses with naked knees and showy petals, glistening bulbous eggplants, burger-size tomatoes. Tinkering with plants during the last hundred years has changed modern life as profoundly as any Detroit motor. So it's a little jarring to realize that in the current world of gardening, a small revolution insists on going in the opposite direction.

Iris reticulata bloom amid snow flurries in the early spring.

Stroll through a rock garden these days and nearly every plant is called a species plant. That means it's the original Charles Darwin plant as designed by nature. Hardy survivors beat out other plants because they adapted to the soil, rainfall, aridity, sun, shade, wind—and nearly every pest.

"That doesn't mean that a species plant is always easy to grow," says rock gardener Bob Nold. "They can be demanding about their conditions." After all, Colorado is filled with pockets of microclimates that allow plants to specialize, adapting so perfectly to defined conditions that they won't grow well anywhere else.

Except in a rock garden, where a specific microclimate is replicated. (Rock gardeners take great pains to use just the right soil, cold, wind, and water conditions that exist in nature.) Flush with bloom in the early spring, the flowers may not be showy specimens like a hybrid tea rose or peony. That's one characteristic of species plants. They come from nature as nature intended.

"It's the chamber music of the horticulture world," says Panayoti Kelaidis, curator of plant collections at the Denver Botanic Gardens. "You don't need the entire orchestra to enjoy a rock garden. Rock gardens are the laboratories of the world's high places."

COLLECTING FROM THE WORLD

That they lend themselves to experimentation is what makes the rock gardens so valuable. These are the gardens where new plants are

Alpines often grow as mat plants, hugging the earth.

introduced to see if they adapt well to a Colorado environment. Are they hardy? Perhaps invasive? This is where plants are tested and found wanting— or successful. In 1980, when Panayoti first began at the Denver Botanic Gardens, he remembers only two penstemon species available at one regional commercial nursery. Although penstemons make up the largest genus of American native wildflowers, it's only recently that they've found themselves as popular in the garden as they are in the wilderness.

Panayoti Kelaidis, curator of plant collections at the Denver Botanic Gardens.

Now you could find a hundred. He also has introduced plants from the Himalayas, Chile, South Africa, the Mediterranean, and the steppes between Turkey and Iran. And, of course, there's the American West. Most are species wildflowers; all are remarkably hardy. "Plants from the steppes make up about a third of the world's plants," he says. The steppes have more than the maritime topography [Europe and the eastern seaboard of America]. And have as many plants in their topography as the tropical rainforests."

Panayoti has collected about fifteen thousand plants, and many have migrated, by way of adventurous gardeners, into regional neighborhoods. These are the plants described as drought resistant, sturdy—even in the face of hail and dipping temperatures—sun loving, alkaline-soil adapted, and impervious to arid winds. A plant that withstands these conditions in eastern Turkey may look just as jaunty in eastern Colorado. It all depends on matching the many microclimates of our state.

"Here in Colorado we need a compass more than green thumbs. The north side of a house is like Alaska, the south almost tropical. You have the acid soil of the peat bogs in Colorado and intensely alkaline soil elsewhere." On one side of a path he points to Himalayan plants, which thrive in acid soil. Just three feet away, the other side contains alkaline soil filled with agaves. Many are botanical postcards from travels abroad.

"At the Denver Botanic Gardens I've been a catalyst more than anything else," Panayoti says about his South African travels to discover new alpines on

Trough gardens create a miniature environment for a collection of plants.

the Drakensbergs Mountains. There, he and a local botanist bounced around in a jeep on a steep dirt road. Together they found an explosion of flowers both in bloom and dripping with seed heads. The blooming flower made the plant identifiable. The botanist shook seeds from the dried heads into an envelope.

Now it's blooming in the alpine section of the Denver Botanic Gardens. Panayoti spreads out his arms as if to take in the thousands of species: "I am a plant Balzac," he says, referring to the French nineteenth-century author renowned for his appetites, "a real plant pig. And you can write that down."

CREATING A PRIVATE LABORATORY

Bob is wandering through his backyard garden. On a day with snow flurries, he's wearing a T-shirt, much too excited about an emerging plant to notice the cold. His two border collies pad along crushed gravel

Crocus buds join succulents on a berm covered by crushed rock.

paths. A small crescent of buffalo grass serves as lawn. It's really for the dogs, because most of the yard is made up of rocks and berms, which are raised mounds of earth.

Small bulbs push through the chilled berms. Cushion plants hug the soil; they are various species, like sea thrift or a cianthus with the look of a hedgehog. Silvery, furry, or succulent leaves indicate that the plant retains moisture. Some leaves are spiky; others creep around rocks like a mat. "We can grow almost all rock-garden plants from around the world," Bob says. Indeed, he's trying just that. Dozens of concrete troughs are filled with unusual varieties of diminutive plants.

"Rare columbines that people can't grow anywhere else can do well here. Rain in the winter can be fatal to these plants, while snow is fine. Alpines don't require a lot of water because the alpine environment is, in effect, a desert. When you say you're an alpine gardener, it doesn't mean you're growing only plants above timberline. Alpines have a definition: under a foot tall."

Alpine life is harsh. These dwarfed plants are stunted naturally to prevent wind or hail damage and to conserve water. Perhaps it's *Rosa woodsii,* a delicate Colorado mountain rose, or a tiny phlox found on Loveland Pass. Their taller brethren live elsewhere.

The Epicenter of Rock Gardening

Rock gardeners may be as varied as classical musicians, mountaineers, famous explorers, or philosophers. It's a pursuit that attracts unbridled individualists.

Alpine plants sprout from a crevice between rocks.

Rather than the lush, brilliant pairings of color in a perennial garden, rock gardeners revel in the architecture of rocks and foliage. In Colorado, rock gardens provide year-round interest in a climate that promises a brief summer.

"Rock gardens are the free verse of the plant world compared to the sonnet of the formal garden. Rock work is bold," Panayoti says.

European rock gardening first began in grottoes where rocks and plants were arranged in a naturalistic setting—the perfect place for a brooding Romantic poet. Later, the asymmetry of the Japanese garden or the studied outline of a Chinese landscape painting was introduced. "They're where the Oriental and occidental influences came together in the nineteenth century. And, in my opinion, the only combination of East and West that truly works," he adds.

In recent times, the epicenter of rock gardens has shifted to Czechoslovakia.

"The Czechs were subjected to fierce treatment by the Russians," Panayoti says. "A lot of people who might have been entrepreneurs became artists—and one of

Cushion plants creep over rocks.

those arts that thrived was horticulture. They still are the biggest plant explorers. They have access to Russia and know how to collect all over the old Soviet Union. They have the precision of the Germans, the passion of the Slavs."

The Denver Botanic Gardens hosted the first rock gardeners from Czechoslovakia in 1986, and the two have been in a close relationship ever since.

Getting Started

The Czechs built rock walls and nestled alpine plants in between the rocks. That set the style and standard for rock gardens around the world. The gardens are a diminutive attempt to re-create the natural terrain. The rocks symbolize mountains. But a rock garden needn't have rocks at all. Berms will elevate the plants for excellent drainage. Bob gathered discarded sod from his neighbor's lawn, layering the rotting grass in piles. Then the berms were covered with small pea gravel for added drainage.

Small bulbs poke through cacti.

Bob flips through the pages of a book written by two Czech gardeners who sell seed. He originally wanted a lush English garden but soon realized that Denver's weather isn't conducive to creating a London setting. Instead, he discovered the North American Rock Society, then the Alpine Garden Society in England, and finally, the Scottish Rock Garden Club. He went on to write a book called *Penstemons* (Timber Press, 1999) and grow thousands of tiny plants in his small backyard.

His advice to would-be alpine gardeners: "First you discover the plant societies, then you discover the great people who are willing to share. Then you discover that your lawn can be turned into berms. And that, well, that's just the beginning."

Panayoti is looking over a new trough garden at the Denver Botanic Gardens. His wife, Gwen, has designed each concrete container, some the size of bathtubs, to reflect a mountain in Colorado. "And here is Mount Evans," he says, gesturing toward the mountain disguised as a miniature landscape. "Over there is southeast Colorado," and the mountains suddenly are reduced to slivers of shale.

Alpines are the understated plants of the horticultural world, perfectly adapted to a harsh environment.

On a chilly spring day, the cushion plants hug the rocks and miniature buttercups or daisies wave bravely in the breeze. It would be easy to overlook these tiny beauties while strolling along a mountain trail. Here, set in a trough as a diamond is set in a ring, their charms are revealed.

The other gardens lie dormant from winter, although some small bulbs have opened under the shelter of trees. But the rock garden heralds the beginning of rebirth in full bloom. Low-key and reserved, the first blush is never bombastic, but a quiet awakening that begins in the higher altitudes, long before the rest of us notice the advent of spring.

NATIVES

Erigeron chrysopsidis var. *brevifolius:* 'Grand Ridge' can be found on the Wallowa Mountains in Oregon. It has bright yellow daisies over a dark green cushion and blooms for months. Three by five inches.

Eriogonum ovalifolium: Although located throughout the West, it can rarely be found in nurseries—but it often is sold as seed. It has dense, silvery cushions of rounded leaves with spherical flowers ranging from pure white to pink, red, and bright yellow and orange. Five by eight inches.

Heuchera pulchella: These miniature coralbells from the Sandia Mountains of New Mexico have large, bright pink bells on very short stems. Five by six inches.

Penstemon caespitosus: Bright blue flowers on spreading, prostrate silvery mats bloom in late spring. Two by ten inches.

Phlox dougiasii: 'Crackerjack' is a hot magenta creeping phlox. Two by eight inches.

EXOTICS

Androsace villosa: From the Alps, this is a tiny alpine jasmine with pure white fragrant flowers. Three by five inches.

Dianthus alpinus: From the Alps, this is a dazzling bright rose flower with intricate speckling in the center. Three by eight inches.

Gentiana acaulis: From the Alps, this is a gentian with cobalt trumpet flowers. Three by eight inches.

Papaver alpinum: From the Alps, the plant's filigree silver foliage has flowers of white, rose, yellow, or orange. Five by six inches.

Primula marginata: This plant has powdery foliage with toothed leaves and cool blue primroses in early spring. Three by seven inches.

RESOURCES

Many seeds for alpine and rock garden plants may be obtained from these plant societies. If you prefer to begin with plants, Bob Nold recommends visiting regional nurseries that carry rock-garden plants that have been thoroughly tested at the Denver Botanic Gardens. Here are some of his favorite alpine and rock-garden society websites:

Alpine Garden Society, AGS Centre, Avon Bank, Pershore, Worcestershire, WR10 3JP, United Kingdom; www.alpinegardensociety.org.

Denver Botanic Gardens, 1005 York Street, Denver, 80206; 720-865-3500; www.denverbotanicgardens.org. The Rocky Mountain Chapter of the North American Rock Garden Society meets at the Denver Botanic Gardens.

The North American Rock Garden Society, P.O. Box 67, Millwood, New York 10546; www.nargs.org.

Prague Czech Rock Garden Club, Klub skalnickaru Praha, Marikova 5, 162 00 Praha 2, Czech Republic; www.backyardgardener.com/cz.html.

CREATIVE SOLUTIONS:

HOMES AND GARDENS
OF THE FUTURE

■ The Farmhouse:
Everything Old Is New Again

by HEIDI V. ANDERSON

She calls it her blue jeans house. It's all about comfort. Open and full of light. Easy to clean. Cool in the summer and warm in the winter. And—something important in Colorado—it's dog friendly.

The Farmhouse is built mostly from recycled materials.

Composed almost completely of bio-based, energy-efficient, recycled, and reused materials, the home makes a statement. It's a model for anyone wishing to reconsider traditional construction. Built from natural products, the architect calls her home The Farmhouse.

It's Not Easy Being Green

Julee Herdt is an architect and assistant professor at the University of Colorado at Denver. Quite a few years ago, the self-described green evangelist realized she would have to leave her profession or learn to create buildings that were less harmful to the planet. With the help of grants from the U.S. Department of Agriculture, she began to develop environmentally friendly building materials. Her most recent project, which was started in 2000 and is designed in conjunction with architect Steve Gates, is the approximately 3,700-square-foot Farmhouse (4,700 square feet with the basement), where she lives with her husband.

At first glance, The Farmhouse looks like any other normal house with a well-designed layout. Walk into a main living area with an open kitchen and doorway out to the backyard. A stairway takes you upstairs to the bedrooms, home offices, and outdoor decks. But look a little closer, and you'll see unique features.

For instance, the kitchen cabinets are made of a mixture of soy adhesives and sunflower plants—you can see the bits of sunflower seeds if you know what you're looking for. The downstairs bathroom—wheelchair-accessible, of course—has as its doorstop a detergent lid. And some cabinets are recycled from the old Boulder Bandshell, a fixture in the community for years for pop music concerts. "A lot of old hippie butts sat in your cabinets," one of the contractors told Julee.

Julee Herdt's spare interior is collected from recycled materials.

The one-of-a-kind home is due in large part to the materials Julee has chosen to use. Consider the flooring, for instance. The linoleum looks like, well, linoleum. But it's a special type, made by a company called Forbo. Forbo flooring is manufactured from a mixture of linseed oil, the most important raw material for linoleum and derivation of the word *linoleum*. It also includes finely ground limestone, cork flour (in some Forbo products), rosin, wood flour, organic pigments, and jute. All the products in Forbo linoleum are almost inexhaustible, naturally raw, and require a relatively small amount of energy for extraction.

Kitchen cabinets are made from a mixture of sunflowers and soy.

Move up from the flooring and you'll see glass tiles. Made of 100 percent recycled glass, these tiles from Sandhill Industries come in a wide range of colors, including pale blue, bright yellow, and deep green. According to Sandhill Industries, the glass tiles are stronger than ceramic tiles and are impervious to water, so they can be used in countertops, showers, and landscaping. And, unlike typical glass tiles, these have a glossy surface rather than a matte finish. Plus, the National Center for Environmental Research touts Sandhill Industries' process for manufacturing paving products. Made from 99 percent recycled soda-lime plate or container glass, they note that the glass pavers are thinner, lighter, denser, stronger—and perform better in paving applications than brick or concrete.

Environmentally friendly products are incorporated behind the scenes, too. Peer under the sinks and take a look at the flexible plumbing. Much of the house

Julee collects examples of building materials that use recycled items.

uses IPEX's Kitec, a composite pipe made of an aluminum tube bonded between two layers of plastic. Because it's bendable, it's relatively easy to install and requires fewer fittings than a traditional system. It's color coded, with orange for hot water (it can handle up to 125 psi at 180 degrees) and blue for cold (up to 160 psi at 140 degrees).

But these pipes are not just for running water between sinks and showers and toilets. The Farmhouse has radiant heating, meaning that these pipes carry water throughout the flooring of the house to help modify room temperature. The heating and cooling system is a geo-exchange system: it transfers heat from deep in the ground below, where it is approximately 50 degrees all year long. That can help cool the house in the summer and heat it in the winter. Additional heat comes from a photovoltaic (solar energy panel) system. Even the lawn mower is solar powered!

The walls, not surprisingly, are also highly energy efficient, thanks to the use of structural insulated panels, or SIPs. SIPs are sandwich panels produced at a factory and shipped to the house for easy assembly. The outside walls use SIPs from Premier Building Systems, the largest SIP manufacturer and exporter in North America. The panels, which are made of expanded polystyrene surrounded by two sheets of engineered wood, are remarkable for insulation ability, strength, fire resistance, and smoothness (no shrinkage because of drying), and they snap together in minutes.

DESIGN FOLLOWS
ENVIRONMENTAL PRINCIPLES

It isn't just the materials that make this house an environmentalist's dream. It's also the overall design.

Windows are from commercial buildings.

For example, consider water use. The lawn is drought-tolerant for low water use and little maintenance. The gutters funnel water into the backyard to water the trees and lawn. And forget about a hot-water heater, which encourages the user to waste water while waiting for hot water to travel from tank to sink. The Farmhouse uses the Metlund system, which circulates the ambient temperature water in the hot water pipes (water that is normally lost down the drain) back to the water heater.

A downstairs bathroom is made up of discarded fixtures.

The design has been modified during the construction process, in part to take advantage of reusable materials Julee discovered along the way. She had originally planned on using huge steel beams for structural support. But when a nearby boathouse was being torn down, she jumped at the chance to salvage its wooden beams. And on the first floor, underneath a stairway, you'll notice a door that is quite narrow. Julee had planned on a larger door, but when that particular one came her way, she found a way to incorporate it into her home.

Julee works in a loft next to a wall that once was a rock-climbing wall in a gym.

The house is still under construction, and that suits the residents just fine. Parts of The Farmhouse have intentionally been left unfinished so that visitors can see its components, such as the insulation materials in some of the walls. Julee is also experimenting with the right paints (including the nontoxic AFM Safecoat line) to see how they work on the various cabinets, countertops, and walls.

Given the unconventional approach to this home, you might expect that it would cost much more than a typical home. Not so, Julee says. It cost about $65 per square foot to build, which is far below the average price of building a new home in Boulder. Some estimates place that figure so far between $100 and $150 per square foot. And the cost of running the house is minimal; heating costs are estimated at about $500 per year.

A Plan for the Future

Clearly, this is the dream house of a dedicated environmentalist. But Julee notes that others who are considering ways in which to make their homes more environmentally friendly don't need to go to extremes to do something good for the Earth.

"If hundreds of people come through this home, and ten get ideas they can use, that helps," she says. "It's a unique home, but I hope it won't be so unique in the future."

A sink is improvised with a ceramic bowl.

RESOURCES

■ ENVIRONMENTALLY FRIENDLY BUILDING PRODUCTS

American Formulating and Manufacturing (AFM), 3251 3rd Avenue, San Diego, California 92103; 619-239-0321; www.afmsafecoat.com. Nontoxic building products.

Forbo Linoleum, P.O. Box 667, Humboldt Industrial Park, Hazleton, Pennsylvania 18201; 570-459-0771; www.forbolinoleumna.com.

IPEX Multipurpose Piping, 9940 East Forty-seventh Avenue, Denver, 80238; 303-754-0102; www.pexinc.com/kitec.html.

Metlund Systems, 3176 Pullman Street, Suite 119, Costa Mesa, California 92626; 800-638-5863; www.metlund.com. Energy-efficient hot-water systems.

Premier Building Systems, 0472 Original Road, Basalt, 81621; 970-927-8400; www.pbspanels.com. Structural insulated panels.

Sandhill Industries, 1896 Marika Road, No. 5, Fairbanks, Alaska 99709; 907-451-6508; www.sandhillind.com. Sandhill glass tiles are carried by Country Floors at Materials Marketing Corp., 600 South Broadway, Denver, 80209; 303-777-3607. Also see National Center for Environmental Research report on Sandhill tiles; http://es.epa.gov/ncer_abstracts/sbir/01/phase1/pollutionverby.html

■ XERISCAPE: PROVIDING A COLORADO "SENSE OF PLACE"

by NIKI HAYDEN

If you think *Xeriscape* sounds like a nonsense word, well, you're right. In 1981, the Denver Water Department struggled to coin a term for drought-tolerant plantings. Overnight, *Xeriscape* came into our vocabulary.

Xeric means "dry" in Greek, but landscape architects tell us that it's simply the wise use of water. The concept has caught on with environmentalists, water conservators, low-maintenance gardeners, and landscape architects.

Most refer to Xeriscape landscaping as providing a regional sense of place. "If you look at old pictures of Colorado, there are no trees, or they're in the low spot," says landscape architect Paula Schulte. "So, to carpet with bluegrass and trees, that's not the Front Range. The xeric principle is to group plants together of similar water needs. Cluster the trees and create a little swale with them where you're going to sit outside. But you don't just dot them all over the landscape. Then you need some open space with grasses. If you go up a little elevation and look east, you can see clusters of shrubs, then clusters of trees, then sweeps of ankle-high grasses."

Drought-resistant plants combined with a few slightly thirstier perennials create a richly textured waterwise garden.

Xeriscape may have caught hold most firmly in New Mexico, where native landscape blends with the homeowner's design uniquely suited to a dry landscape. But in Colorado, designing with Xeriscape principles requires reconsidering Kentucky bluegrass lawns. It's possible to mix plantings that require less water with areas of water-guzzling lawn or vegetable gardens.

Landscape architects approach a xeric design with common principles. First, they group heavy-water lovers together and lay down drip irrigation or sprinklers. That includes those lawns, vegetable gardens, and traditional perennial or annual beds that demand a lot of water. Then they group the medium-water lovers together on a separate watering system. That might include many trees and flowering shrubs. Finally, they'll group xeric plants where the sprinkler doesn't reach. Perhaps it's that difficult strip of dirt between the sidewalk and the street. Or maybe there's a corner where irrigation never reaches.

Hardy purple ice plant, (*Delosperma cooperi*), produces a low-growing mat of succulent leaves that spreads vigorously.

When it comes to finding plants for that xeric space, "the first thing to do is to find plants that aren't very choosy," says Jim Knopf, Xeriscape landscape architect and author of two Xeriscape books. "Most will grow in clay or sand."

If you're new to Xeriscape and want to try it, horticulturists offer a few suggestions.

Start with a plan. Where do you want turf? If you live close to the foothills, receive adequate snowfall, and have trees that shade the afternoon sun, then Kentucky bluegrass may be best for you. If you live on the Colorado plains, where the soil is baked each summer, consider buffalo grass (for heavy clay soils), or a bunch grass such as blue grama (for sandy soils). Surround your turf with resilient trees, shrubs, and flowers.

Choose the right plants. Most garden centers group xeric plants together. Separate your water-loving plants, such as vegetables, from xeric plants. Or integrate water-loving annuals and perennials with vegetables.

Xeric plants combine with vivid colors and mid-summer blooms.

Amend your soils differently. Vegetables will need what some landscape designers call "chocolate cake soil." This is high in organic matter, manure, mulch, and fertilizers. Xeric plants need slight amending—especially in new developments where the topsoil has been scraped off. They don't need rich, loamy soil but they do need good drainage. Consider adding mulch such as three-eighths-inch gravel instead of wood bark.

Avoid overwatering. Xeric plants often are killed by too much kindness. Remember that many are native to Colorado or originate in arid climates such as the Mediterranean, South Africa, or Turkey—areas similar to our own with cold winters, little rainfall, and brisk winds.

AN INTERVIEW WITH JIM KNOPF

Jim Knopf is the author of Waterwise Landscaping with Trees, Shrubs and Vines: A Xeriscape Guide for the Rocky Mountain Region, California and the Desert Southwest (*Chamisa Books, 1999), which is a companion to his first book,* The Xeriscape Flower Gardener: A Waterwise Guide for the Rocky Mountain Region *(Johnson Books, 1991). A landscape architect specializing in Rocky Mountain Xeriscape design, Knopf also serves as a consultant to regional water boards.*

Front Range Living (FRL): How would you describe our weather, soil, and water conditions here on the Front Range?

Jim Knopf (JK): Weather—we've got the wildest stuff on the planet. It's so changeable because our mountains run north to south. In contrast, mountains in Asia run east and west and block that extreme weather, while ours is wildly fluctuating.

The U.S. Department of Agriculture zone system, which is almost like a mantra, doesn't really work west of the Mississippi. They try to predict weather based on the average minimum temperature, which is unpredictable here. So try to find a geographic location where a plant grows well. If it grows well in Rapid City, South Dakota, it will grow well here.

Another way to look at gardening in our area is that we're at a pioneering stage. Here, you can play with new plants.

FRL: Vegetable gardens, you point out, do need what you refer to as the "chocolate cake soil" to thrive. This would be a loamy mixture of compost, leaf mold, aged manure, and possibly peat moss. All the vegetable gardening books tell us how to go about preparing that soil. Xeric plants prefer a leaner soil; often, you say, a clay soil. How would the Front Range gardener go about designing soil for xeric plants? And once you have amended the soil and planted, do you need to fertilize?

Russian sage *(Perovskia atriplicifolia)*, a newcomer to Colorado, has proved to be a tough landscape shrub that blooms in late summer.

JK: You don't need to design the soil. The first thing to do is to find plants that

The delicate chocolate flower *(Berlandiera lyrata)* on its wiry stem rises from a small mat of leaves.

aren't very choosy. Most will grow in clay or sand. We've got all kinds of gravel, rock, and sand in the floodplains, and clay pockets. And there are all kinds of clay. It's a myth that everyone has clay. There are people in Louisville on either clay or sandy loam. Topsoil can be wonderful soil if it hasn't been taken away.

Soil may differ in parts of the yard; just dig a hole and examine the soil. If it's crusty, take a closer look—that will have to be

Although most commonly known yarrows (*Achillea* spp.) are a bright yellow, several now can be found in varying colors from to pink, purple and white.

amended. For most of us, a soil test isn't necessary. If you suspect heavy clay, pour in a bucket of water and it will sit for days. You'll know what you've got. Also, compost doesn't always last very long.

In alkaline conditions, organic materials disappear so quickly. This is provocative in gardening. Organic amendments work best in a chocolate cake soil. The topsoil of subdivisions is a mineral soil, but if it's been scraped away, you'll have to add some kind of topsoil. Go out to a garden center and touch and feel the loamy soil. It is useful to stick your hand in it.

Here are a couple of basics: try to pick plants that aren't fussy about their soil. You can run into problems with wet clay, but with most xeric plants, you don't have to worry about it.

FRL: Which is better for a Front Range lawn, blue grama grass or buffalo grass?

JK: Buffalo grass has little runners that spread. Blue grama is a bunch grass. If you want wildflowers in a natural meadow, then blue grama is better. If you want a traditional lawn, buffalo grass is the answer. It likes clay and really doesn't like fancy soil.

On the Front Range, we're at the border where buffalo grass thrives, which is on the plains. Use

Blue grama grass (*Bouteloua gracilis*), the state grass of Colorado, forms distinctive "eyelashes" by the height of summer.

it where the soil is heavy clay on a south-facing slope. Closer to the foothills like Boulder and Colorado Springs, bluegrass, a cooler grass, works. So buffalo grass isn't best for everything, but it's best for hot, dry areas.

I like tall fescue. It's important to talk about turf types of tall fescue. I find that it does use less water. It is a grass that requires irrigation, but it just requires less irrigation than bluegrass. Aim for half the water of bluegrass. Tall fescue will grow right up to the trunks of ponderosa pines, and it competes with shrubs and is tougher in the shade than bluegrass.

Snow-in-summer *(Cerastium tomentosum)* companions with a perennial geranium 'Johnson's Blue'.

FRL: Can you plant a front yard in all perennials? If so, would it be more or less tolerant than a low-water turf such as buffalo grass? Would a xeric yard be better with a mix of plants, trees, and grasses?

JK: Industrial strength perennials will grow in the same conditions as buffalo grass, although perennials will tolerate a little more watering. If you're keeping it xeric, the grass [buffalo grass] won't come back. But if you want to mix xeric perennials and buffalo grass lawn, do the edges first. Don't place the xeric plants right next to the lawn. Plant intermediate plants at the transition, like daylilies. Creeping mahonia is another one. Snow-in-summer is too close to the ground and you get a tangled mass.

FRL: Probably the most important, and hardest, concept to master is to place plants of like needs together. Describe how a garden might be divided between high-water-need plants and low-water-need plants.

JK: The first thing is to group plants with water needs and soil needs. In California I've got two examples. In one case they're working hard to understand

Moonshine Yarrow (*Achillea* x 'Moonshine') has become a predictable companion to Russian sage.

the needs of every plant and running irrigation to every plant. That's a lot of work. In the second, they're putting plants of similar needs together. Three groups are sufficient. More than that and it's too complicated.

FRL: What is the best way to keep weeds down in a xeric landscape?

JK: The strategy is to have as little bare ground as possible. Find plants that you really like for those places. Experiment. Find what will fill that space. Find the plant to fight the war for you rather than the chemicals.

FRL: What native plants thrive in our gardens? What imported plants thrive? Are garden centers carrying greater varieties of these plants, or do we have to find suppliers?

JK: You can get junipers everywhere. The really good news is that if you write down the name of the plant, your garden center will have it next time. Garden centers have gotten into being the first to have these things. Some do a lot of the growing themselves. Also, you can call on the phone to the wholesale person and then call the garden center and ask them to add it, or piggyback it, to their order. More and more people are doing this.

FRL: Any last suggestions?

JK: It would be great for garden centers to put color tags on water needs so customers would know how to group them. In the West, we have advantages with low-water and high-water plants. We've only just started finding our own way. You do get a lot of variety in a dry space. There are always going to be disappointments with a cold wave. But every year is so different. This isn't a bad place to garden; it's just different.

Jim Knopf's Industrial-Strength Perennials

Arizona zauschneria
(*Zauschneria arizonica*)

Basket-of-gold (*Aurinia saxatilis*)

Bearded iris (*Iris germanica* cvs.)

Broom groundsel (*Senecio spartioides*)

Buchara iris (*Iris bucharica*)

Centranthus (*Centranthus ruber*)

Chocolate flower (*Berlandiera lyrata*)

Coronation gold yarrow (*Achillea filipendulina*)

Crocus species (*Crocus* spp.)

Daffodils (*Narcissus* spp.)

Dotted gayfeather (*Liatris punctata*)

Double bubble mint (*Agastache cana*)

Faassen's catnip (*Nepeta faassenii*)

Hardy pink ice plant (*Delosperma cooperi*)

Lavenders (*Lavandula* spp.)

Maximilian's sunflower (*Helianthus maximilianii*)

Moonshine yarrow (*Achillea* x 'Moonshine')

Moss phlox (*Phlox subulata*)

Native four o'clock (*Mirabilis multiflora*)

Native gaillardia (*Gaillardia aristata*)

Pineleaf penstemon (*Penstemon pinifolius*)

Fischer sage (*Salvia azurea* var. *grandiflora*)

Poppy mallow (*Callirhoe involucrata*)

Porter's aster (*Aster porteri*)

Prairie zinnia (*Zinnia grandiflora*)

Rocky Mountain penstemon (*Penstemon strictus*)

Russian sage (*Perovskia atriplicifolia*)

Santolina (*Santolina chamaecyparissus*)

Sea lavender (*Limonium latifolium*)

Snow-in-summer (*Cerastium tomentosum*)

Soapwort (*Saponaria ocymoides*)

Popular Xeric Trees, Shrubs, and Flowers Believed Hardy in Colorado

Except for piñon pines and junipers, very few trees grow in near-drought conditions. These tough specimens will require some regular watering.

Trees: piñon pine *(Pinus edulis)*; western hackberry *(Celtis reticulata)*; amur or ginnala maple *(Acer tataricum* sp. *ginnala)*; ponderosa pine *(Pinus ponderosa)*; golden raintree *(Koelreuteria paniculata)*; bur oak *(Quercus macrocarpa)*; Gambel oak *(Quercus gambelii)*

Shrubs, grasses, and flowers form the backbone of drought-tolerant gardens. These require moderately low to very low watering.

Shrubs: various junipers; fernbush *(Chamaebatiaria millefolium)*; silver buffaloberry *(Shepherdia argentea)*; rabbitbrush *(Chrysothamnus nauseosus)*; Apache plume *(Fallugia paradoxa);* gray santolina *(Santolina chamaecyparissus);* yarrow *(Achillea filipendulina);* leadplant *(Amorpha canescens)*; curl leaf mahogany *(Cercocarpus ledifolius)*; lilac *(Syringa vulgaris* and *Syringa* x *persica)*; Russian sage *(Perovskia atriplicifolia)*; Western sand cherry shrub *(Prunus besseyi)*; blue mist spiraea *(Caryopteris* x *clandonensis)*; Harison's rose *(Rosa* x *harisonii)*; Austrian copper rose *(Rosa foetida bicolor)*; Spanish gold hardy broom *(Cytisus purgans)*

Bulbs: crocus, species tulips

Herbs: garden culinary sage *(Salvia officinalis)*; English lavender *(Lavandula angustifolia)* and its many varieties; Provence lavender *(Lavandula* x *intermedia)*

Ground covers: creeping mahonia *(Mahonia repens)*; pussytoes *(Antennaria)*; woolly thyme *(Thymus lanuginosus)*; Mexican evening primrose (*Oenothera speciosus*—can be invasive); basket of gold *(Aurinia saxatilis)*; moss phlox *(Phlox subulata)*; snow-in-summer *(Cerastium tomentosum)*; Claude Barr's mat penstemon *(Penstemon caespitosus)*; Turkish speedwell *(Veronica liwanensis)*; compact sea pink *(Armeria maritima)*

Flowers: sulphur-flower *(Eriogonum umbellatum)*; orange globe mallow *(Sphaeralcea munroana)*; dwarf silverleaf marguerite daisy *(Anthemis biebersteiniana)*; butterfly weed (*Asclepias tuberosa*—hard to transplant, try growing it from seed); purple prairie clover *(Petalostemon purpurea)*; white bouquet tansy *(Tanacetum niveum)*; Jupiter's beard *(Centranthus)*; yarrow *(Achillea filipendulina* 'Moonshine'); salvia *(Salvia nemerosa)*; Rocky Mountain penstemon *(Penstemon strictus)*; pink hardy ice plant *(Delosperma cooperi)*; cranesbills geraniums *(Geranium species)*; coreopsis

(Coreopsis grandiflora); gaillardia (Gaillardia aristata); blue flax (Linum perenne); Mexican hat coneflower (Ratibida columnifera); double bubble mint (Agastache cana); prairie winecups (Callirhoe involucrata); Missouri evening primrose (Oenothera missouriensis); silver speedwell (Veronica incana); red rocks penstemon (Penstemon x mexicali); Spanish Peaks foxglove (Digitalis thapsi); Maximilian's sunflower (Helianthus maximiliani); blue catmint (Nepeta x faassenii); chocolate flower (Berlandiera lyrata); dotted gayfeather (Liatris punctata); sea lavender (Limonium latifolium); native four o'clocks (Mirabilis multiflora); pineleaf penstemon (Penstemon pinifolius); prairie zinnia (Zinnia grandiflora); bearded iris (Iris germanica)

Grass: turf-type tall fescue (Festuca elatior); buffalo grass (Buchloë dactyloides); blue grama (Bouteloua gracilis, a bunch grass)

Ornamental grasses: little bluestem (Schizachyrium scoparium); Karl Foerster feather reed (Calamagrostis arundinacea); blue avena grass (Helictotrichon sempervirens); prairie sky switch grass (Panicum virgatum); silver beardgrass (Andropogon saccharoides); prairie dropseed (Sporobolus heterolepis)

RESOURCES

■ GARDEN DECOR AND SUPPLIES

Echter's Greenhouse and Gardens, 5150 Garrison Street, Arvada, 80002; 303-424-7979; www.echters.com. Pottery and general garden supplies

Tagawa Garden Center and Florist, 7711 South Parker Road, Aurora 80016; 303-690-4722; www.tagawagardens.com. Pottery and general garden supplies

■ HELPFUL ORGANIZATIONS

Denver Water Office of Conservation, 1600 West Twelfth Avenue, Denver, 80204;

303-628-6343; www.denverwater.org. Xeriscape tips.

Xeriscape Colorado! Inc., P.O. Box 40202, Denver, 80204; www.xeriscape.org.

Xeric basics and information on xeric demonstration gardens.

■ MAIL-ORDER NURSERIES

Colorado garden centers are providing more xeric plants than ever. But if you can't find what

you need, try these:

High Country Gardens (Santa Fe Greenhouses), 2902 Rufina Street, Santa Fe, New Mexico

87505; 800-925-9387; www.highcountrygardens.com. Santa Fe nursery that offers both

Colorado and New Mexico xeric plants.

High Country Roses, Split Mountain Garden Center, 9211 East U.S. Highway 40, Jensen, Utah

84035; 800-552-2082; www.highcountryroses.com. Source for hardy roses acclimated to the

Rocky Mountain climate.

■ RECOMMENDED READINGS

Waterwise Landscaping with Trees, Shrubs and Vines: A Xeriscape Guide for the Rocky

Mountain Region, California and the Desert Southwest by Jim Knopf (Chamisa Books, 1999).

The Xeriscape Flower Gardener: A Waterwise Guide for the Rocky Mountain Region by Jim Knopf

(Johnson Books, 1991).

Xeriscape Plant Guide: 100 Water-Wise Plants for Gardens and Landscapes by Denver Water

(Fulcrum Publishing, 1996).

Xeriscape Handbook: A How-to Guide to Natural Resource-Wise Gardening by Gayle Weinstein

(Fulcrum Publishing, 1999).

■ BRICK BY BRICK: BUILDING WITH ADOBE

by NIKI HAYDEN

At the foot of a bluff in Trinidad, Colorado, Jennifer Green's adobe house is near completion, a new house in a region that has birthed adobe homes for more than one hundred years. The canyon is rescence to a peaceable kingdom of wildlife, horses, dogs, and a tabby cat as well as a landscape of cacti, sagebrush, and yucca. Using her own hands, the petite third-grade teacher shaped, hoisted, and placed brick after brick and now knows the painful truth about adobe dwellings: "They're cheap, but labor intensive," she says grimly. "You're better off with a crew."

Dirt cheap. Jennifer's adobe came from the dirt under her house, a four-foot crawlspace. Earth was dug and sifted for rocks and debris, then mixed with water and straw. Wet mud was poured into eighteen-by-twenty-four-inch molds, allowed to firm, and then pulled free. Jennifer scraped any jagged edges and left the bricks to dry—all 2,100 of them. "You pull the mold off and the bricks remain to cure until it dries. You do have to cover them from the rain. You come to know the power

Adobe bricks line up after drying in the sun.

of water, which is both your friend and your enemy," she says. Besides a sifter, made from wire screening, and a wooden mold, you need only a trowel to apply a finishing coat of mud slurry.

It's a beautiful and romantic building material, so elemental that it's easy to imagine anyone could make adobe. After all, adobe is an ancient method for building in the Southwest, and similar methods are found around the world. "When I moved to Trinidad eight years ago, I was set to buy a house, but the deal fell through. First I built a shed of adobe. Then, a chicken house. Eventually, I was

Adobe bricks with new windows await a slurry of adobe mud as a plaster.

in way over my head. You can't imagine the complexities of a house," she says. And then there were all the cuts, bruises, and sore muscles that accompany the construction.

She first put in vinyl windows, then tore them out and replaced them with wood. Electrical wiring runs under the floor rather than through the walls. Colorado code required treated wood everywhere the wood touched the adobe—a useless reasoning, she says, since very old adobe homes and their wooden windows remain in excellent condition. And she settled on a woodstove rather than trying to run heat throughout the house. The hurdles were jumped; then came the rains.

PRESERVING ADOBE FROM HARSH WEATHER

Torrential downpours pelted Jennifer's house. Trinidad is on the border with New Mexico and shares a similar climate. It's an alpine desert where cacti bloom. Storms arrive quickly, lashing out with fury and then quickly subsiding. Arroyos carved into the landscape by flash floods indicate what rain will do to adobe. Once Jennifer's house was finished, with two coats of finely strained adobe mud on the outside, a deluge of rain created pock-marked rivulets into the exterior walls. She was horrified.

"This is controversial," Jennifer says, "but I added a layer of Portland-based plaster on the outside." The color of the house changed from brown to gray.

Jennifer embedded fossils into the drying adobe slurry.

Traditionally, layers of adobe slush would be spread over the bricks to bake in the sun until they dry to a rigid mud skin.

"Women would refinish the exterior each year, in a traditional house," Jennifer says, "but it's a lot of work." The stucco has problems of its own, she adds. In the 1920s, homeowners placed chicken wire over their adobe homes and spread stucco over the wire and exterior. Sometime later they discovered that the adobe inside simply washed away, leaving a stucco shell behind.

Jennifer isn't sure that her method will be successful. The unpredictable weather forced her into a quick decision. But this is the same climate that makes adobe attractive. Trinidad is hot in the summer, cold in winter, and arid. The surrounding hard-packed clay of the land also transforms into adobe as durable as the bricks that line the streets of Trinidad. The small city is famous for brick and rock work of all kinds. Adobe simply came first.

An adobe wall has a tiny niche cut out. Thick glass blocks serve as windows above.

"Wouldn't you want adobe?" Jennifer asks, and runs her hands along a smooth adobe wall with the texture of unglazed pottery. "It's the most forgiving of all materials. Put a nail in the wall to hang a picture. If you change your mind, you can just remove the nail, spit on some earth, and patch the hole."

Even the binder for adobe can adapt to include horsehair or pine needles rather than straw. But as elemental as adobe may be, those skilled in the craft are dwindling in number. There are secrets to the masonry, Jennifer says, and one of those essential bits of knowledge is to understand the touch and feel of earth—enough clay, enough sand—to form good-quality bricks.

TURNING TO HISTORY

Jennifer turned to the Baca House, one of a series of museums in Trinidad owned by the Colorado Historical Society. The Baca House is adobe, built in

The Baca House is a combination of adobe and gingerbread trim.

the territorial style of 1870. It's a brilliant combination of American and Hispanic influences that date to Fort Union, north of Santa Fe, New Mexico, just after the Civil War. The two-story white-gingerbread-trim Greek Revival house with peaked roof is American. The adobe is Hispanic and Native American, with walls twenty inches thick. Together, they form a stylish hybrid.

For decades, master craftsman Manuel Gamboa has cared for the Baca House's adobe shell inside and out, with its lustrous exterior and whitewashed interior. He first worked on it in 1966 when it was part of the museum complex but also the private home of the director. Everyone in Trinidad knows, Jennifer says, that Manuel is the expert. Paula Manini is director of the museum and says that Manuel has lived in Trinidad for thirty-five years, but was originally trained in adobe work by his father in Chihuahua, Mexico.

"I was nine years old when I started working with my father," Manuel says. It was in an area of Mexico much like Trinidad. The trees, crops, and weather patterns are nearly identical. The soil, too, proved to be good adobe material.

Manuel brings dirt from the Spanish Peaks to the Baca House for his adobe slurry. It's from a ranch that has the dirt he likes. "He can squeeze it with his hands and knows exactly what it needs. He applies it the old-fashioned way, and it will last. When snow builds up, he'll do some patching. But as far as the whole structure goes, it has lasted," Paula says.

"We looked all over," he says, "trying dirt from many areas. But dirt from the Spanish Peaks was the best. I call it the grain—how it feels in my hand—the right amount of sand to dirt." If the clay and sand aren't mixed in the right proportions, the adobe will crack. Too much clay and you'll have to add sand. Too much sand, you'll have to add clay. Finding the correct mixture in nature will save hours of labor. This dirt has little or no humus, or organic material, that would be suitable for farming. Instead, it's perfect for making bricks.

He also prefers ryegrass to any other kind of straw. It's best at the end of the season when the grass has dried and cattle have walked on it, he says. That way, it's nearly threshed and ready to be crumbled.

But Manuel is less concerned about rain with adobe. A solid roof, he says, that's the most important way to protect adobe. Manuel believes the greatest threat to the Baca House came from gutters in disrepair that let in the rain, not weather on the outside walls. "How adobe lasts depends on how much protection it has," he says. "Here, in Trinidad, we have to put on a new coat of adobe every five to six years."

Manuel is familiar with using a cement plaster on the outside, but sighs over the consequences. It will eventually crumble, he believes, and turn to powder. Instead, he relies upon a thin, hard last coat—perfectly constructed to seal the house like a membrane. The exterior slurry is made the same way as the bricks, but the

The backyard of the Baca House is home to a traditional garden with heirloom vegetables.

screen mesh is finer. The dirt that filters through is as powdery as silt. Straw is chopped until nearly the consistency of hair. Then a layer is applied with a trowel and allowed to dry.

THE SPIRIT OF AN AGE

Adobe is the product of a self-sufficient age. Paula notes that Trinidad was on the Santa Fe Trail, which originated as a highway for commerce, not pioneers. Spain limited any trade between its northern colonies and the outside world, but when Mexico broke away from Spain, trade opened doors. Trinidad was born. "People were grateful for manufactured goods," Paula says, and factory blessings like tin roofs perfectly suited their handmade adobe homes.

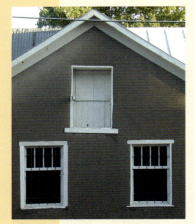

Outbuildings once housed workers, now they serve as a museum complex.

The Baca House is exquisite, a simple structure with the charm of white icing on gingerbread. It's modest by today's standards, but was a showpiece in its day. One year after it was built by a Pennsylvania couple, Felipe and Dolores Baca bought the home for seven thousand pounds of wool—the basis of their family fortune—and moved in with their nine children. One year later, Felipe died.

The house became Dolores's, and her spirit remains. Her children grew up to become highly educated, respected citizens. Dolores attended to the family business and immersed herself in church and civic causes. The Baca House survived disrepair, the Great Depression, and a murder upstairs in 1945—a grim litany of unloving owners. "Still, it has a bright and inviting atmosphere," Paula says, perhaps because Dolores's imprint was stronger than later misfortune.

Trinidad is filled with unique architecture. Like a laboratory of masonry, you'll see buildings of sandstone rocks and elegant brickwork. Workers from eastern Europe and Italy have added touches through the decades. The Baca House is one of these jewels, and a reminder that adobe once flourished as a building material in Colorado.

Jennifer decided to heat her home with a wood-burning stove.

If adobe weren't so forgiving, Paula points out, the Baca House would not have survived. It has never been covered by anything other than mud. And the homes of the household workers, housed in a traditional one-story adobe structure behind the home, remain as well. The dwellings went through rough time in the last hundred years, but stand intact.

"Not everyone will like this work," Paula admits. "You're up to your elbows in mud. No one wants to work that hard." But Paula lists other adobe houses in Trinidad that now are covered over by siding. You would never guess they were adobe, but at one time they formed entire neighborhoods of adobe homes.

OLD AND NEW

Like Jennifer's home, the Baca House is heated by wood-burning stoves. Inside the Baca House, the whitewashed walls look like crisp linen. Wood ceilings are painted a sage green, and the floors are wooden planks. Jennifer's home is distinctly modern and features several inside walls that are adobe. She has taken advantage of the drying process to embed fossils, block-glass windows, tile, and small niches. The curve of adobe walls is elegant, and the broad windowsills hold potted plants.

While the Baca House includes a formal parlor and family parlor, Jennifer's living space is a living room and study combined. The kitchen is large enough to include a dining table. The Baca House offers a small, cramped

The Baca House out-buildings have small wood windows.

kitchen that was closed off in the summer, when the outside *horno*, or adobe oven, could be substituted.

Upstairs, the Baca House is a series of bedrooms for children. Jennifer's upstairs is one large bedroom.

You won't find a bathroom in the Baca House. The privy was outside. Jennifer's bathroom is lined with colorful tiles inserted directly into the wall.

Gardens catch the last rays of summer with heirloom varieties of squash, corn, tomatillos, beans, peppers, hollyhocks, and tansy in the Baca House backyard. The walkway to Jennifer's front door is paved with flagstones, and, instead of the traditional *horno*, there's a modern outdoor grill.

Times and trends have changed, but adobe continues. "Where I grew up in Mexico we had the same weather as Trinidad—very dry but with terrible rainstorms," Manuel says. "But the house that my great-grandfather built was still standing. It was two hundred hundreds years old. Adobe can last forever."

RESOURCES

■ HELPFUL ORGANIZATION

The Earthbuilding Foundation, Inc., c/o P. G. McHenry, 5928 Guadalupe Trail Northwest, Albuquerque, New Mexico 87107; 505-345-2613; www.earthbuilding.com. Nonprofit that includes architects and builders who encourage adobe and rammed earth buildings. In conjunction with the University of New Mexico, offers workshops and books on building with adobe.

■ MUSEUMS

Baca House, 300 East Main Street, Trinidad, 81082; 719-846-7217; www.coloradohistory.org/hist_sites/trinidad/bacahouse.htm. Part of the Trinidad Museum complex, which also includes the Bloom Mansion, a Victorian. Open May through September.

Bent's Old Fort, 35110 Colorado Highway 194 East, near La Junta, 81050; 719-383-5010; www.nps.gov/beol. Adobe structure reprised as it was originally; located at original site.

El Pueblo Museum, 119 Central Plaza, Pueblo, 81003; 719-583-0453;
www.coloradohistory.org/hist_sites/Pueblo/pueblo.htm. Adobe trading post reprised on its 1842 site.

Fort Vasquez Museum, 13412 U.S. Highway 85 (one mile south of Platteville), Platteville, 80651;
970-785-2832; www.coloradohistory.org/hist_sites/ft_vasquez/ft_vasquez.htm. Adobe fort.

Meeker Home Museum, 1324 Ninth Avenue, Greeley, 80631 970-350-9220. Two-story adobe
home built in 1870 for Nathan C. Meeker, founder of Greeley.

■ RECOMMENDED READING

Living Homes by Suzi Moore McGregor and Nora Burba Trusson (Chronicle Books, 2001).
Includes four contemporary adobe homes in Colorado.

■ WEBSITES

Adobe Builder, Attn.: Joe Tibbets, P.O. Box 153, Bosque, New Mexico 37006; 505-861-1255;
www.adobebuilder.com. Extensive information on adobe building.

This Old House, P.O. Box 62376, Tampa, Florida 33662; www.thisoldhouse.com. Site of the
popular television show informative page on adobe

APPENDIX

COLORADO HISTORIC HOMES

■ ADOBE HOMES AND FORTS

Baca House, 300 East Main Street, Trinidad, 81082; 719-846-7217; www.coloradohistory.org/hist_sites/
trinidad/bacahouse.htm. Part of the Trinidad Museum complex. Open May through September.

Bent's Old Fort, 35120 Colorado Highway 194 East, near La Junta, 81050;
719-383-5010; www.nps.gov/beol. Adobe structure reprised and built to be historically
accurate. Located at the original site.

Fort Vasquez Museum, 13412 U.S. Highway 85 (one mile south of Platteville), Platteville, 80651;
970-785-2832; www.coloradohistory.org/hist_sites/ft_vasquez/ft_vasquez.htm. An adobe fort.

The Meeker Home Museum, 1324 Ninth Avenue, Greeley, 80631; 970-350-9220. Two-story
adobe home built in 1870 for the founder of Greeley, Nathan C. Meeker.

El Pueblo Museum, 119 Central Plaza, Pueblo, 81003; 719-583-0453;
www.coloradohistory.org/hist_sites/Pueblo/Pueblo.htm. The 1842 adobe trading post
reconstructed on its original site.

■ ANCIENT HOMES

Mesa Verde, near Cortez and Mancos in southwest Colorado, 81330; 970-529-4465;
www.nps.gov/meve. U.S. National Park of 52,000 acres; contains dwellings of ancient people
dating from about a.d. 600 to a.d. 1300.

■ ARTS AND CRAFTS

Boettcher Mansion, Lookout Mountain Nature Preserve, 900 Colorow Road, Golden, 80401;
303-526-0855; http://ww2.co.jefferson.co.us/ext/dpt/comm_res/boettcher. Arts and crafts style
from 1917.

Hoverhome, 1309 Hover Road, Longmont, 80501; 303-774-7810; www.stvrainhistoricalsociety.org/
Hoverhome.htm. Large Tudor-style home with arts and crafts interior. Beautiful stained glass
of yellow roses became a theme throughout the house: yellow roses on china, yellow roses
planted out front.

■ CABINS

Colorado Chautauqua Association, 900 Baseline Road, Boulder, 80302; 303-442-3282;
www.chautauqua.com. A collection of turn-of-the-century cabins that once formed a
Chautauqua—a gathering place for cultural events and summer getaways.

Enos Mills Cabin, 6760 Colorado Highway 7, Estes Park, 80517; 970-586-4706.
Cabin of Rocky Mountain National Park's founder.

Hiwan Homestead Museum, 4208 South Timbervale Drive, Evergreen, 80439; 303-674-6262;
http://ww2.co.jefferson.co.us/ext/dpt/comm_res/openspac/hiwan.htm. A nineteenth-century log
home furnished in the style of the 1920s and 1930s.

■ COTTAGES

McAllister House Museum, 423 North Cascade Avenue, Colorado Springs, 80903;
719-635-7925; www.oldcolo.com/~mcallister. Victorian Gothic cottage from 1873.

Pearce-McAllister Cottage, 1880 Gaylord Street, Denver, 80206; 303-322-1053;
www.coloradohistory.org/hist_sites/Pearce/p_Mcallister.htm. Dutch colonial revival from 1899
that houses the Museum of Miniatures, Dolls and Toys.

■ VICTORIAN

Arnett-Fullen House, 646 West Pearl Street, Boulder, 80302; 303-444-5192; www.historicboulder.org.
Tiny gingerbread Victorian full of whimsical touches. Historic Boulder home.

Astor House Hotel, 822 Twelfth Street, Golden, 80401; 303-273-3557.
www.astorhousemuseum.org. Originally an 1867 hotel that became a boardinghouse,
the Astor House was built from native stone.

Avery House, 328 West Mountain Avenue, Fort Collins, 80521; 970-221-0533.
Locally quarried sandstone home with Queen Anne touches, built in 1879.

Bloom Mansion, 300 East Main Street, Trinidad, 81082; 719-846-7217. Part of the
Trinidad Museum complex. An extravagant mansion with remarkable brickwork.
Open May through September.

Byers-Evans House Museum, 1310 Bannock Street, Denver, 80204; 303-620-4933.

Restored Victorian mansion with many of its original furnishings.

Colorado Governor's Mansion, 400 East Eighth Avenue, Denver, 80203; 303-866-3682.

Colonial revival home; offers guided tours.

Grant-Humphreys Mansion, 770 Pennsylvania Street, Denver, 80203; 303-894-2505.

Beaux-arts home built 1900 to 1902.

Hamill House, Argentine and Third Streets, Georgetown, 80444; 303-674-2625.

Victorian home built in 1867 and expanded upon for two decades by a wealthy mine owner. One of a five-house historic district that features distinct classes in the mining town. Included are the Bowman–White 1892 Italianate home of a wealthy mining entrepreneur, the modest Kneisel House of a merchant's family, the Tucker–Rutherford Cottage, which was a miner's home, and the very early rustic Johnson Cabin, constructed by a prospector.

Healy House Museum and Dexter Cabin, 912 Harrison Avenue, Leadville, 80461; 719-486-0487; www.leadvilleusa.com/history/healy.htm. Greek revival Victorian mansion that celebrates the silver rush in Leadville. Inside is much of the history and lore of the silver barons, H. A. W. and Augusta Tabor. Alongside is a rough-hewn cabin.

Molly Brown House, 1340 Pennsylvania Street, Denver, 80203; 303-832-4092; www.mollybrown.org. Home of Colorado's famous Titanic survivor.

The Rosemount Museum, 419 West Fourteenth Street, Pueblo, 81003; 719-545-5290; www.rosemount.org. Stunning Victorian from 1893.